For Those Who Have Run Dry

Cycle A Sermons
For Pentecost through Proper 16
Based On The Gospel Texts

David Kalas

CSS Publishing Company, Inc.
Lima, Ohio

FOR THOSE WHO HAVE RUN DRY

FIRST EDITION
Copyright © 2022
by CSS Publishing Co., Inc.

Library of Congress Cataloging-in-Publication Data

Names: Kalas, David, author.
Title: For those who have run dry : cycle A sermons for Pentecost through proper 16 based on the gospel texts / David Kalas.
Description: First edition. | Lima, Ohio : CSS Publishing Company, Inc., [2022]
Identifiers: LCCN 2022020043 (print) | LCCN 2022020044 (ebook) | ISBN 9780788030543 | ISBN 9780788030550 (ebook)
Subjects: LCSH: Bible. Matthew--Sermons. | Pentecost season--Sermons. | Common lectionary (1992). Year A.
Classification: LCC BS2575.54 .K35 2022 (print) | LCC BS2575.54 (ebook) | DDC 226.2/06--dc23/eng/20220624
LC record available at https://lccn.loc.gov/2022020043
LC ebook record available at https://lccn.loc.gov/2022020044

For more information about CSS Publishing Company resources, visit our website at www.csspub.com, email us at csr@csspub.com, or call (800) 241-4056.

e-book:
ISBN-13: 978-0-7880-3055-0
ISBN-10: 0-7880-3055-8

ISBN-13: 978-0-7880-3054-3
ISBN-10: 0-7880-3054-X

PRINTED IN USA

Contents

The Holiday For Those Who Have Run Dry

Marriage counselors will sometimes talk to couples about making emotional deposits and withdrawals. The idea is that we human beings are finite creatures, and even the most stable and good-natured soul does not have a limitless reservoir of energy, good cheer, and hope. When the people or circumstances around us keep making "withdrawals," therefore — drawing down and draining our energy and emotions — we will eventually come to a point where we feel like we have nothing more to give. It's important for husbands and wives, therefore, to do the little things that serve as "deposits" in their spouses.

We know the truth of it, and it goes beyond marriage. The same phenomenon occurs in the workplace, at school, and at church. Most of us are not able to maintain completely separate compartments of energy and emotion, and so both the "withdrawals" and the "deposits" can come from almost anywhere in our lives. And perhaps we know well the feeling that we have run dry; that we have nothing more to give.

That's a painful place to be. It means that we have already experienced some kind of cumulative drain, very probably over the course of a long time. So many concerns that we've been carrying, so many needs that we've been meeting, so many difficulties arise that have conspired to erode away our smile and *joie de vivre*. Then, to compound it all, we may also feel guilty, for we sense that we are failing those around us. We are curt instead of patient, cynical instead of hopeful, weary rather than robust, and glum instead of ebullient.

Today, then, is the holiday for us.

Today is the Day of Pentecost — the annual Sunday when we recall and celebrate the coming of the Holy Spirit. Typically, when we think of that occasion, we remember the story of the events of the day as recorded in Acts 2. But there are other passages that also prompt us to affirm and celebrate the coming of the Spirit.

Perhaps we should begin, however, by acknowledging the implications of our Christian holy days. Most holidays, both secular and sacred, are remembrances of things that happened in the past. It is not a uniquely religious pattern. That is what is at stake when we celebrate Independence Day, for example, or the birthday of some significant person from history, or even just the anniversary of our marriage. Holidays are typically remembrances of something that happened in the past.

When we Christians, therefore, set aside special days each year to celebrate as holy days, we are almost always pointing to a past event. Most notably, we remember and celebrate the birth of Jesus, his triumphant entry into Jerusalem, his last supper, his crucifixion, and his resurrection. Perhaps we also mark special days to remember and celebrate his baptism and his transfiguration. After all of those annual celebrations, we also recall and celebrate the coming of the Holy Spirit.

The critical question with each commemoration, however, is this: What does that event from so many years ago have to do with me today?

I have a pretty good sense for the continuing relevance and impact of, say, Independence Day. The births of certain historical figures may feel somewhat more remote. Then there are these biblical events — placed further back on the timeline than probably any other holiday we celebrate. What is their contemporary and personal relevance?

The answer to that question may vary with the individual. There is, in the Christian holy days that we celebrate, a tremendous range of potential. On the one hand, these biblical events may seem as far removed from our daily life as the day Caesar crossed the Rubicon: historically significant, but personally irrelevant. Or, on the other hand, they may feel as personally impactful as the day we got married or the day our child was born.

Consider, for example, how we sing about some of our holidays. Reflecting on the birth of Jesus, for example, and mindful of the gifts presented to him by the Magi, Christina Rossetti asked, "What can I give him, poor as I am?"[1] No one sings about what they can do to help Alexander the Great against the Persians.

On Palm Sunday, we may sing together, "Into the city I'd follow the children's band, waving a branch of the palm tree high in my hand."[2] That's a very personal approach to an event that occurred 2,000 years ago. Does anyone sing about being part of a parade in Babylon honoring Nebuchadnezzar?

Even more dramatically, the old spiritual asks, "Were you there when they crucified my Lord?"[3] Beyond the first century, that would be a silly question to ask anyone. Do we sing to one another, "Were you there when Booth shot Lincoln?" Yet the holy days commemorating these biblical events have this potential for being intimately personal.

The great difference between Caesar crossing the Rubicon and these several biblical events that we've mentioned is that there is a real opportunity to appropriate the biblical events and make them our own. They may be transferred from the pages of the history book into our own personal scrapbook. They become events in our lives to the extent that we recognize and embrace them as events that are meant for us.

John Wesley, in his famous Aldersgate experience, testified, "An assurance was given me, that he had taken away my sins, even mine, and saved me from the law of sin and death."[4] In that moment, the cross of Christ was no mere historical event; now it was a personal event for Wesley. The thing that happened so long ago in the past changed his life in the present.

And then what of the holy day that we celebrate today? The annual Day of Pentecost affirms the coming of the Holy Spirit.

1   Christina Rossetti, "In the Bleak Midwinter," UMH #221 in the public domain

2   William H. Parker, "Tell Me the Story of Jesus," UMH #277 in the public domain

3   "Were You There When They Crucified My Lord," UMH #288 in the public domain

4   John Wesley, *The Works of John Wesley*, Third Edition, Volumes 1, (Grand Rapids: Baker Books, 1996), p.103.

Is that for us a remote, historical event, like Caesar crossing the Rubicon? Or does it have something to do with us in a personal and daily way?

Interestingly, our selected scripture for today is not from Acts 2, which is scripture's account of the Day of Pentecost. Instead, we read from an episode in John's gospel, recording an event from Jesus' earthly ministry. In the midst of a great crowd gathered for an annual festival, Jesus called out this invitation: "If any man is thirsty, let him come to me and drink. He who believes in me, as the scripture said, 'From his innermost being shall flow rivers of living water.'" And then the narrator of the gospel added this explanatory word: "He spoke of the Spirit, whom those who believed in him were to receive; for the Spirit was not yet given, because Jesus was not yet glorified."

Jesus' open invitation, you see, included an anticipation of the coming of the Spirit, but the Spirit had not yet come as of at that moment. The Spirit's coming was later. But Jesus looked ahead to that good gift in this passage, just as he does in several other places (such as Luke 11:13; 24:49).

When the Spirit did come, for whom was the Spirit given? The passage is perfectly clear about the answer. "He spoke of the Spirit, whom those who believed in him were to receive." That is why Jesus' invitation is to come to him, for it is in and through him that we receive the gift of the Spirit. And that gift of the Spirit, Jesus says, is an inner experience, which he says is like "rivers of living water."

Two other times in John's gospel — both during Jesus' conversation with the Samaritan woman at the well — this expression of "living water" was used. But in addition to the references in John's gospel, the expression seems to find its antecedent in the Old Testament. Through the prophet Jeremiah, the Lord referred to himself as "the fountain of living waters" (Jeremiah 2:13). And in the prophet Zechariah, there was a someday promise of "living waters" that would flow out of Jerusalem to the east and to the west.

"Living" is not typically the descriptor that we attach to "water." We may think of cold water or of fresh water, but not *living* water. To the people of that ancient world, however, the image was a meaningful one, indeed. Water was a precious commodity, which was sometimes hard to come by; and the people of Israel were also acquainted with water that was "dead."

Just a few miles to the east of Jerusalem lies the Dead Sea. It was not called by that name in Bible times, but its name was the next best thing: the Salt Sea. The Dead Sea is notoriously salty — with many times greater salinity than the Great Salt Lake in the United States — and its dense mineral content results in an environment that prevents plants and animals from being able to flourish there. Consequently, the Dead Sea is a startling sight to a visitor — a large body of water surrounded by desert. The Dead Sea would be a rude disappointment to any visitor who was thirsty, for its water is undrinkable, bringing death rather than life.

Most of us live in situations where we can take water for granted. It is available with the simple turn of a knob in multiple rooms in our house. There is no trekking down to the well or the creek in order to lug back buckets of water — let alone a concern lest the well run dry, and a new one would need to be dug.

The people in Jesus' audience, by contrast, had a much more precarious relationship with water. It was just as essential to life as it is for us today, but not nearly so easily accessed. If anything, homeowner's insurance premiums may discourage us from living too near to water, but in the ancient world living near water was a necessity. And "living water" was especially to be desired.

The idea of living water, you see, stood not only in contrast to the dead waters of the Salt Sea. It also represented a contrast from other sources of water that people in that world used. Certain wadis or streams, for example, would routinely run dry during predictable seasons of the year. And the cistern, of course, was a finite container for water, which could eventually be emptied by use.

In the aforementioned reference to living water that the Lord spoke through Jeremiah, he lamented, "My people have committed two evils: They have forsaken me, the fountain of living waters, to hew for themselves cisterns, broken cisterns, that can hold no water" (Jeremiah 2:13 NASB). Two contrasting sources of water, you see: cisterns and living water.

The "living water" did not refer to water that was somehow magical, like some conception of Ponce de Leon's Fountain of Youth. No, it simply referred to flowing water — a reliable stream that never runs dry. The cistern is finite — and, in the case of the people of Jeremiah's day, cracked. But the "living water" is infinite. The cistern can be emptied by our repeated withdrawals, but we may draw from the living water again and again forever.

So it is with the Holy Spirit, whom Jesus gives to all who believe in him. Jesus promises an experience of something that "shall flow rivers of living water." This is a resource that will not fail us, like a shallow wadi, in the dry season. And this is a source that will not be depleted by our daily dependence on it.

It was no doubt this empowering of the Spirit that prompted Paul to declare, "I can do all things through him who strengthens me" (Philippians 4:13 NASB). It was this supernatural source that gave Stephen both boldness and peace in the face of his opponents. It was this uncontainable blessing that so spilled over from Peter that even his shadow brought healings (Acts 5:15).

By ourselves, human beings are finite. We are limited, indeed. We cannot afford to have the world around us making constant withdrawals from us. We also need deposits.

But that suggests that our only resource is a cistern. And Jesus has something more and better for those who belong to him. "Rivers of living water" — a gushing superabundance, that is not from us or from the people around us, but from the Spirit within us. And he, his coming, and his presence are what we affirm, celebrate, and rejoice in this holy day!

Amen.

Trinity Sunday
Matthew 28:16-20

A Family Picture

No family picture is complete.

Perhaps you have seen one of those special family portraits that are sometimes taken during a fiftieth wedding anniversary or some such. Perhaps you've even been part of one. Seated in the center are the proud patriarch and matriarch, surrounded by their adult children, plus grandchildren, and perhaps also great-grandchildren. It endeavors, of course, to be a complete family portrait. And it may well be that the whole family is there for that occasion.

Yet, still, it is never a complete family picture, is it? We can think of the family members who have gone before who are no longer with us. We can imagine the family members who will marry into and be born into the family in the coming years. It may be a snapshot of the moment, but it is not a complete family picture, for the whole family is not together. They never are. Not this side of heaven, at least.

Every family photo, therefore, has a bittersweet quality to it. Scour the photo albums and scrapbooks, and in every instance you will discover the same thing. People are missing. Such is the changing nature of life on this earth.

The gospel reading from the end of Matthew is like a family snapshot of a moment, but it, too, is not a complete picture.

The scene is a mountain in Galilee. "Mountain" might be something of a misnomer for folks who live in places where there are genuine mountains, which stretch above the tree line and disappear into the clouds. Galilee doesn't have mountains like that. But the region does feature a lot of hills, some of them with spectacular views of the water, fields, and valleys below.

There, atop one such hill, the risen Christ appears to his disciples. And we read in this concluding passage from Matthew's gospel Jesus' familiar great commission. These are the Lord's marching orders as the story transitions from his own earthly ministry to that of his disciples.

"Disciples" are the key to this family photograph. Matthew referred to "the eleven disciples," which naturally brings to mind that someone is missing from this picture. We are accustomed to thinking in terms of Jesus' twelve disciples, after all — not eleven. Indeed, each of the four gospel writers at various times refer to the disciples collectively as "the twelve." This reference to "the eleven disciples" reminds us that someone is missing from this family picture. Judas was no longer with the group.

We all know the poignancy of the vacant chair. The family member who is suddenly no longer with us. The friend who was always there, but now is gone. And when we have a get-together that the person would ordinarily have been a part of, we feel their absence very deeply.

I have to imagine that is how the disciples felt. You and I may easily write off Judas because his reputation preceded him in our minds. From the first moment his name appeared in any of the gospels, we reckon him as a villain. Yet surely that was not how the disciples felt about him. Indeed, it would hardly have qualified as betrayal if he had been recognized as an enemy, or even an antagonist.

But that's not what Judas was — not, at least, until the very end. Rather, he was part of their group. He was, literally, one of their number. And it had only been a matter of days before that the surprising and tragic events of Maundy Thursday had occurred. When the eleven disciples gathered with Jesus on that mountain, therefore, there must have been a terrible sense of vacancy. It was a group picture, but with a conspicuous absence.

On the occasion recalled here by Matthew, Jesus had an instruction for those eleven disciples. We remember that, elsewhere, he told them, "As the Father has sent me, I also send you" (John 20:21 NASB). This "great commission," then, is the substance of his sending. He commanded the eleven disciples, saying, "Go therefore and make disciples of all nations."

The reference to the Father sending the Son directs our attention to the very center of this family portrait. In our liturgical calendar, today is identified as Trinity Sunday, and our passage from Matthew recalls the truth of the Trinity in the specifics of Jesus' instructions about making disciples. "Baptizing them," Jesus said, "in the name of the Father and the Son and the Holy Spirit." This family photo is not ultimately about us. We owe our place in this picture — our role in this family — to the Father, Son, and Holy Spirit.

The very mission on which Jesus was sending his disciples involves all three persons of the Trinity, as well. As we noted above, the whole sending enterprise is the Father's gracious initiative in the first place. These sent ones, then, are to go and tell all nations about the Son and teach them to obey his commands. We discover in Luke that the disciples are not to embark on their mission until after the Holy Spirit had come upon them. "You are to stay in the city," Jesus told them after his resurrection, "until you are clothed with power from on high" (Luke 24:49 NASB). The Father sends the Son; the Son sends the disciples; and the Spirit empowers them for their divine mission.

Meanwhile, we are struck by the evolution in how Jesus expressed the mission for his followers. When he first called Peter and Andrew, you recall, he said, "Follow me, and I will make you fishers of men" (Matthew 4:19 NASB). We might reasonably assume some parallels between "fishers of men" and "make disciples of all nations" — that is to say, Jesus had an eye on a larger "catch" from the beginning to the end. Yet still we see that a shift took place.

First, we observe that Jesus spoke always in a language that his audience understood. While "disciple" was not a foreign word in the context of first-century Palestine, these men had not yet been taught about and experienced what it was to be disciples of Jesus. They had experienced fishing, however. The initial invitation was expressed in terms of being "fishers." It was only after several years of being discipled by him, then, that Jesus was able to speak to them of 'making disciples.'

That, in turn, led to the second shift that took place: a shift in agency. In our English translations the verb "make" appears in both passages, but the subject of that verb changes from the call scene to the sending scene. When Jesus called them to follow, he promised, "I will make..." When he sent them out, however, he commanded them to "make." He had trained them for their task; now it was time for them to complete that task.

There is something beautifully organic about this instruction that we refer to as the Great Commission. He was speaking to "the eleven disciples," and he told them to go and "make disciples." In other words, they were to reproduce. They were to make more of what he has made them.

This, then, is yet another way in which we see that the family picture of Matthew 28 was not complete. Just as the whole family was not there because one of their members — Judas — was no longer with them, so, too, the whole family was not there because there were so many more yet to be born into that family. Whole nations remained to be made into disciples! Matthew's language ("the eleven disciples") and Jesus' commandment ("go... make disciples") both tell us that this family photo is a snapshot, but there are a lot of people missing.

When we look through our own family scrapbooks and photo albums, we are immediately aware of who is missing from each picture. I wonder, though, if we have the same sensitivity to God's family. In this matter, we pray that he would create his own heart within us so that we might see as he does.

Our Lord, you know, is so marvelously aware of who is missing. He is the shepherd who counts the sheep, and is not content to have almost all of them. Instead, he ventures out to search for the one lost lamb. He is, likewise, that woman who turns her house upside down to recover the coin that was missing. He does not simply write-off the loss. And, above all, he is the father whose every impulse is to welcome, rejoice, and celebrate when the missing son returns home.

In that third parable, the story of the prodigal son, you remember that the older brother in the family was not equally pleased by the prodigal's return. Indeed, he was quite unhappy about the party being thrown to celebrate the sibling-scoundrel.

And so it seems that, while the father was understandably grieving until his younger son returned home safe and sound, the older son was content with his younger brother missing.

Will you and I be characterized more by the father's heart or by the older son's? Will we be discontent and grieving until all God's children are home? Or will we be complacent and indifferent about the multitudes who are missing from the family picture?

The scene from Matthew 28 is like a family picture. As such, it is beautiful. But it is also incomplete.

If we take the same picture today, the look would be very different. Unless you have a very special lens — one that sees beyond this visible world — those original eleven disciples will not appear in the family photo that would be taken today. But see how many, many millions of faces are part of the picture now! They are of every age and station. They are of every size, shape, and color. They are from all around the globe. And they are all descendants on the family tree, tracing their lineage back to the first recipients of the great commission.

As members of that family photo today, you and I are the contemporary recipients of that commission. Do we sense that? Do we recognize that the great commission originally spoken to Peter and Andrew and the rest is also spoken to us? In the military, it might be called "standing order." It is the mission to be accomplished until the commander himself supersedes that command.

More than just a standing order, it is the characteristic will of God. In the Garden of Eden, you remember, the Lord expressed his desire that his creatures should reproduce. "Be fruitful and multiply," he said to both man and beast. His design, you see, was that they should go and make more of what he had made them. That was the essence of his word to the first humans and animals. And that was also, you see, the thrust of his word to the eleven disciples. He had made them into disciples; they were to go out into the world and make more of what he had made them.

All these generations later, that is surely his word to us. Inasmuch as this is typical of his will and his design, we may count on it that this is what the Lord has in mind for us. Let us not succumb to the world's mistaken notions about Jesus, Christianity, evangelism, or the gospel. Let us, rather, be the ones who see clearly the heart of God and the will of God, in order that we may obey the command of God.

First, see what he has made you. Whatever it is, rejoice in it, for that is your testimony. It is also what you are uniquely equipped to accomplish in the lives of others. He sends you out to reproduce that good work of his grace.

And, second, see the family picture. It's a beautiful scene, to be sure, but it is incomplete. There are folks missing. The Father misses them, and he has tasked you and me with the loving vocation of bringing them into the family and bringing them into the picture.

Amen.

Proper 3 (8)
Matthew 6:24-34

The Surprising Case Of Master Mammon

The New Testament world was a world of slaves and masters.

As a small piece of sample evidence, we might note this. The English translation of the New Testament contained in the New American Standard Bible features over one hundred references to slaves and slavery. The entire New Testament only has 260 chapters, which suggests that slavery was a prominent theme.

Furthermore, though it is sometimes an offense to our modern sensibilities, those dozens of references to slaves and slavery are not diatribes against the practice or editorials advocating for the emancipation of slaves. Those who long for Jesus and the apostles to appear in the text as crusaders against the institution of slavery will be disappointed.

Of course, as with so many themes, there is a great difference between reporting a practice and endorsing that practice. The Old Testament narrators, for example, report a great many instances of polygamy, but those accounts should not be equated with an approval of men having many wives. On the contrary, a careful reading of the narratives almost always reveals that polygamy did not work out well for those involved.

So, too, the New Testament has been misunderstood and misused historically by those who have employed it to support the practice of slavery. The fact is that slavery was an enormous factor in the culture of the ancient Mediterranean world — the world from which the New Testament came — so it is bound to play a part in the stories, teachings, and letters of the New Testament. Beggars and lepers are there in abundance, too, but we do not construe that to mean that the New Testament is at peace with poverty and leprosy.

Meanwhile, we must be careful that our modern indignation over the history and practice of slavery not blind us to some larger truths.

First, not all slavery was of the sort that we associate with our own history in the United States. The huge population of African slaves here in America represented a kidnapped people, who were often treated with unthinkable cruelty. Not every slave in the New Testament world fits that profile. Some slaves, in fact, were voluntary slaves, and in that ancient Greco-Roman setting the slave of an important person often enjoyed greater status and more power than the average peasant did, even though the latter was "free."

We may note, for example, how routinely the apostles refer to themselves as bond-servants of Christ (such as Romans 1:1, Galatians 1:10, Titus 1:1, James 1:1, 2 Peter 1:1, Jude 1:1, Revelation 1:1), The underlying Greek word for bond-servant, we should point out, is the same as the word translated elsewhere as "slave." We take it that the term was not one automatically accompanied by bitterness or resentment. No, the apostles no doubt embraced the privilege of belonging to and serving the greatest master of all.

Furthermore, when we read the many references in scripture to slaves and slavery, we should recognize that the Bible is perhaps more matter-of-fact about circumstances in this world than many of us are. The natural human response to an unfavorable circumstance is an impatience to get out of that circumstance. From the time we are children, this is how we react. Yet time and again the testimony of scripture bears witness to a God who works providently in the midst of unfavorable circumstances. His deliverance is much more patient and profound than a mere "get out of jail free" card.

Finally, there is a spiritual reality that must not be overlooked. "Slave" and slavery" are not used exclusively in scripture to refer to the literal practice of one human being owning and controlling another human being. Indeed, one could argue that the prevailing New Testament meaning lies elsewhere.

We think, for example, of how Jesus used the imagery of slaves, servants, and masters to explain discipleship. "Which of you," he asked, "having a slave plowing or tending sheep, will say to him when he has come in from the field, 'Come immediately and sit down to eat'? But will he not say to him, 'Prepare something for me to eat, and properly clothe yourself and serve me until I have eaten and drunk; and afterward you will eat and drink'? He does not thank the slave because he did the things which were commanded, does he? So you too, when you do all the things which are commanded you, say, 'We are unworthy slaves; we have done only that which we ought to have done'" (Luke 17:7-10 NASB).

He also tellingly juxtaposed the disciple-teacher relationship with the slave-master relationship. "A disciple is not above his teacher, nor a slave above his master. It is enough for the disciple that he become as his teacher, and the slave as his master" (Matthew 10:24-25 NASB).

And, as we have already noted, the apostles readily understood themselves as "servants of Christ."

Meanwhile, the other dominant spiritualizing of the slave-master imagery in the New Testament involves the human being's relationship to sin. "Truly, truly, I say to you, everyone who commits sin," Jesus said, matter of factly, "is the slave of sin" (John 8:34 NASB). It was and is a potent image. Jesus' hearers knew how it was to live under the authority and control of a master. They understood being owned by another person and being obligated to serve that person. This, Jesus says, is our relationship to sin. These are slaves that need to be set free, you see.

The Apostle Paul, likewise, made great use of that imagery in his letter to the Romans. He accepted it as a truism that human beings are "slaves of sin," but against that reality proclaims the truth that "our old self was crucified with (Christ), that our body of sin might be done away with, that we should no longer be slaves to sin" (Romans 6:6 NASB). Interestingly, though, Paul's vision was not of a person who went from being a slave to being a free person. Rather, the liberation was simply in becoming a slave with a different master. "Thanks be to God that though you were slaves of sin, you became obedient from the heart to that form of teaching to which you were committed, and having been freed from sin, you became slaves of righteousness" (Romans 6:17-18 NASB).

If Jesus and Paul were correct, then it was not just the first-century Mediterranean world that was a world of slaves and masters. That is our world, too. Indeed, that is our own life experience. We are all slaves, you and I — it is only a question of what master we serve, and to whom we belong.

In light of that, it makes perfect sense that Jesus would declare, "No one can serve two masters." Yet we wonder if that's a false dichotomy. After all, do we have to serve any master? We Americans prize our freedom. As the notion and definition of freedom has become more and more personalized in our culture, we instinctively reject the suggestion that we are slaves with masters. We don't belong to anyone. We don't serve anyone.

Or do we?

We don't need to look far or think long to make a list of ways that people in our world are in bondage. We are people who are slaves to the cruel master of some addiction. We are people who are prisoners of some past hurt or trauma; people who labor joylessly day after day in some job or responsibility. We are people who are chained up by worry, anxiety, or fear. people who are captive to some appetite or ambition, some agitation or discontentment.

We may not be owned by some other human being, but that does not mean that we are truly free. Many of us know what it is to have some "master," and we are ripe therefore for the good news and happy prospect of serving a different one. That is central to the liberated life that Jesus offers us.

In the case of our selected passage from Matthew 6, Jesus singled out a perhaps surprising alternate master. Mammon — or, as some translations render it, "money" or "wealth" or "riches." "You cannot serve God and mammon," he said.

This is a foreign concept to our ears. We think in terms of earning money, saving money, and spending money. Those are the verbs of our vernacular when thinking about our relationship to money. But "serve"? We do not naturally think in terms of "serving" money.

Does that mean that we don't serve money — that we are more free of that master than the folks in Jesus' original audience? Or might the reality be elsewhere? Could it be that we don't recognize our servitude in this area? Could it be that we are unwitting slaves?

We wish that we could ask Jesus the follow-up question. What does it mean to "serve mammon"? How do we know if we are doing that?

Jesus did not leave us hanging. He went on in Matthew 6 to talk about other issues, but perhaps they were not other issues, after all. He encouraged his followers not to "be anxious" for the material needs of life — "what you shall eat, or what you shall drink... what you shall put on." And in order to reassure them, he painted for them a lovely picture of their heavenly Father's provisions for "the birds of the air" and "the lilies of the field."

If these subsequent teachings about worry, food, drink, and clothing were extensions of the original teaching about not being able to serve two masters, then serving mammon hits closer to home.

Perhaps you are acquainted with the parallelism that characterizes biblical poetry. We think, for example, of the first verse in the book of Psalms: "How blessed is the man who does not walk in the counsel of the wicked, Nor stand in the path of sinners, Nor sit in the seat of scoffers!" (Psalm 1:1 NASB). We observe the parallelism of the nouns and verbs in those three phrases. The verbs of walk, stand, and sit echo one another, while the nouns of "the wicked," "sinners," and "scoffers" also serve to inform and interpret one another.

We see that sort of Hebrew poetic way of expressing thoughts in some of Jesus' prose. When he said, for example, "Ask, and it shall be given to you; seek, and you shall find; knock, and it shall be opened to you," (Luke 11:9 NASB), we recognize the pattern. The ideas rhyme. The thoughts echo and reinforce each other.

Perhaps, then, we might understand this passage from Matthew 6 more fully if we read it as Hebrew poetry. Perhaps there is a correlation between the nouns and the verbs of these teachings. When we juxtapose "you cannot serve God and mammon" with "do not be anxious for your life," perhaps we see some parallels. First, there are parallel prohibitions: "you cannot" and "do not." Then come the operative verbs: "serve" and "be anxious" (or, in some translations, "worry"). Finally, we come to the objects of the verbs: "mammon" and "your life," which is elaborated as "what you shall eat, or what you shall drink, (and) what you shall put on."

When we hear Jesus say, "You cannot serve God and mammon," we want to ask, "What does it mean to serve mammon?" But it may be that he has already answered the question. To serve mammon is to worry about your life and its material needs.

Suddenly the teaching becomes a startling declaration. Is it possible that Jesus is telling me that I cannot both serve God and also worry about my life and its material needs? Yet that is precisely what I — and so many American Christians — endeavor to do.

We do not readily think of ourselves worshiping other gods, and we are reluctant to embrace the idea that we serve any masters. But Jesus was challenging us with a spiritual truth. Master is not just a title, it's a relationship. It's not a figurehead; it's a life-changer.

Rather than just assuming that we serve God, that the Lord is our master, perhaps we might take a kind of diagnostic test, instead. Let us ask ourselves the key questions, and let our answers reveal who our master is (or our masters are). Our service, our allegiance, our chief concern, our priorities, and our devotion — these all belong to one's master. And so I ask myself, "Who or what truly gets my service day after day? What has my real allegiance?" Let me candidly list my chief concerns. Let me evaluate what a typical day reveals about my priorities. Let those around me bear witness to what enjoys my fullest devotion.

Like it or not, we live in a world of slaves and masters. The good news is that our Lord wants us to be set free from every other master. He is stunningly, lovingly possessive about you and me. He has paid the price to purchase us so that we might belong — entirely and exclusively — to him.

Amen.

Come, Build With Me

Perhaps you've seen the scene for yourself. Perhaps you've even been a part of it. And even if you haven't, you can easily imagine it. It has happened on family camping trips, youth group retreats, and scouting events. The family, group, or troop arrives at the campsite, and they find themselves unloading and setting up camp in the midst of a torrential downpour.

It's no fun putting up your tent in the rain. The very elements for which you're trying to prepare have already arrived. The tents are going up to keep you from getting wet. But now, instead, you, your tents, and all of your belongings are getting soaked during the very process designed to keep you and your stuff dry. Alas.

There is a great irony in the scene. But in the end, it makes a good story. Even if the participants aren't laughing while they're going through it, you know that they'll all be laughing about it afterward.

Except when it's tragic.

Sometimes, you see, setting up camp in the midst of a storm isn't funny; it's heartbreaking. Sometimes it doesn't make for a good story, because the storm itself is such a painful experience. Sometimes building in the rain is not ironic; it's tragic.

Chapters 5, 6, and 7 of Matthew's gospel are devoted to perhaps the single-most famous collection of Jesus' teachings. Taken together, we know those three chapters as the Sermon on the Mount. They are filled with familiar and profound passages, like the Beatitudes and the Lord's Prayer. Here we read the encouragement to turn the other cheek, the startling challenge to cut out of our lives whatever causes us to sin, the sobering equating of lust with adultery, anger with murder, and the invitation to be perfect as our heavenly Father is perfect. The Sermon on the Mount is filled with rich counsel and counter-cultural demands.

It is the daring recipe for living like Christ's kingdom while still living in this fallen world. At the conclusion of it all, Jesus talked about a storm.

Near the end of Matthew 7, Jesus painted a brief picture of two different housebuilders. The one, according to Jesus, built his house on sand. Then he told us that "the rain descended, and the floods came, and the winds blew, and burst against that house." We are not surprised to hear, then, that this house with so dubious a foundation came crashing down.

The other housebuilder, by contrast, built his house on the rock. That is more promising, to be sure. When Jesus says that "the rain descended, the floods came, the winds blew, and burst against that house," we are unsurprised to hear that the house survived.

Jesus was economical in his storytelling. He sketched the basic outline of the events. But we may use our imaginations — and our experiences — to color in the picture he had sketched. Specifically, we can imagine the experience of each homeowner when the storms came.

There is a marvelous sense of security that comes with being inside during a storm. How many times have we looked out the window at menacing clouds, strong winds, and torrential rains, and felt grateful for the safety and comfort of our homes? Our walls and roofs afford us a feeling of protection and confidence. We read peacefully by the fireplace, while the winds and rain, the thunder and lightning, all rage outside our windows.

Ah, but if the storm is stronger than our house — if the power of nature is greater than the strength of our walls or roofs, our windows or sump pumps — then we are desperate, indeed. This is not the playful stuff of pitching a tent in the rain. When the floodwaters are rising, or when the winds have the force of a tornado or hurricane, then we no longer sit peacefully by the fireplace.

We have seen footage — or perhaps we have experienced for ourselves — the scramble to board windows against the coming hurricane or to pile sandbags in defense against the overflowing river. We know the sound of the sirens, the hurrying to the basement, and the family members clinging to one another in fear of nature's fury.

When the storm is past, we know the look of devastated communities and flattened neighborhoods. Where once was a scene of happy suburbia, with sidewalks, bicycles, and cul-de-sacs, now there is nothing but rubble and heartache.

This is not usually the stuff of having built on sand. This is just the fact of life in this world. Nature has forces that still can exceed our best engineering and construction.

We can color in the picture that Jesus had sketched out for us. We are familiar with the look and feel. We know about both the house that endured a storm and the house that did not. And we can imagine — or perhaps remember — the feeling and experience of both kinds of homeowners.

In the case of Jesus' parable, the houses and their builders are only metaphorical — physical symbols of spiritual realities. The one builder is characterized as wise, while the other is foolish. It turns out that the wisdom or foolishness, along with the accompanying end results, are entirely matters of choice. It is up to us which house we will build and which fate we will experience. "Everyone who hears these words of mine, and does not act upon them," Jesus explained, "will be like a foolish man..." Conversely, "everyone who hears these words of mine, and acts upon them, may be compared to a wise man..."

The sort of either/or choice that Jesus was portraying is reminiscent of the sort of paradigm we find in so many other places in scripture. Jesus was building on a tradition with which his audience was well-acquainted from the Old Testament. Moses, for example, laid out for the people of his day the blessings and the curses that accompany obeying and disobeying God, respectively. It's a matter of choice, you see, and Moses' paradigm is very similar to Jesus'. The idea is that the people had heard the Lord's teaching — in the one case, the Old Testament law; in the other case, the Sermon on the Mount. They knew all that they needed to know, therefore, to live wisely. The vastly different results of living wisely or unwisely are predictable.

We see the same sort of paradigm played out in the world-view of Proverbs. Time and again, the wise, ancient writer portrays the binary choices of life, and he assures his audience of the results of each choice. We may be prudent or rash; disciplined or self-indulgent; humble or arrogant; generous or stingy; and so forth. Day after day, we make these choices. In the end, the Proverbs assure us that a life of rash, self-indulgent, and arrogant decisions will lead to ruin. Conversely, a humble, generous person who is prudent and disciplined will enjoy health and prosperity in the end.

So it is that Jesus, in his story of the two housebuilders, was working with a well-established ethic. The people in his audience were already acquainted with the if-this/then-that counsel of the Old Testament. Jesus was saying that how one responded to his teachings was the key to a happy or unhappy ending.

The noteworthy detail in the story of the two housebuilders, however, was that they both experienced the storm. This was a crucial point. It is easy for a person to feel ill-used when they have tried to do everything right, only to have some calamity befall them. They shake their fist at the injustice of life in this world.

But Jesus was matter-of-fact about the storms. The wisdom of the one housebuilder did not insulate him from the wind and the rain. The difference between the two builders was not that the one had to experience the storms of life, while the other was spared. No, both men were subject to the difficulties that simply come with the territory of life in this world. The difference was not in what they experienced, but in how they survived.

As a pastor, I have watched many people who are living out the painful, real-life version of the otherwise humorous scene of folks trying to put up their tents in the midst of a storm. The tragic variation of it, though, is the person who is trying to build their house on the rock when the wind and the rains are already hammering them. I have seen it again and again, and it breaks my heart. They are people who have not done the work of building their lives on Jesus' words prior to their crisis. And then, in the midst of the crisis, they come to the pastor's study, and they try to start building during the storm.

The wise builder is not immune from having a child who goes astray. She is not guaranteed an easy marriage. He is not spared every accident and disease. The wise builder is not able to build his house in some ideal location that is free from storms.

This was the terrible flaw in the logic of Job's friends. They saw the troubles that had befallen Job, and they concluded that there must have been something wrong with him. If he had been wise and righteous and just, he would have been exempt from the storms. But that was not the paradigm that Jesus taught.

No, the wise builder is not able to build his house in a location that is free from storms. Such an unfallen ideal awaits us in the New Jerusalem. But Jesus promised that the wise builder's house would survive the storms.

How? What was the secret formula for such strength, such viability, such endurance? Just this: hear his words and act on them.

At first blush, such a recipe may not seem sensible. Yet we know the truth of it in other, more mundane areas of life. We think, for example, of the person who sits down to assemble the recently purchased piece of furniture. Many of us have stories to tell about times when we have forged ahead without reading the directions, only to have the final product collapse or turn out quite badly. To heed the words is to guarantee a better assembly.

Parents, too, know the truth of this principle. They know that if their children will just heed their words — their advice, rules, and counsel — things will go better for those kids. As my own children have heard me say many times: "Everything's better when you just obey!"

This is a recurring premise in the Old Testament law, and a paradigm reiterated by the writings and the prophets. If the people of God would simply order their lives according to his statutes and ordinances, they would find that all of life would be blessed. As individuals, as families, and as a society, their "house" would fare better if built on God's words.

We can see the plausibility of Jesus' statement. "Everyone who hears these words of mine, and acts upon them," he insisted, "may be compared to a wise man, who built his house upon the rock. The rain descended, and the floods came, the winds blew, and burst against that house; and yet it did not fall, for it had been founded upon the rock." The task that is ours, therefore, is to build our houses upon that rock.

One of the lovely scenes that all of us have witnessed and in which many of us have participated is the communal effort to set up a campsite. Whether it's a family, a youth group, or a scouting troop, it's a fun, efficient, and satisfying experience when folks are working together to set up their tents. It's often possible, of course, for an individual to do it by themselves. But it is so much more pleasurable — and usually more easy and effective — when folks help each other do it. We notice that the beauty of that scene — the cooperative effort — is always the same, rain or shine.

This, then, is the lovely invitation and opportunity available to the church. Let us be that family, that group, that troop, that builds together. Let us explore with one another the teachings of Jesus, and then let us help each other to apply those teachings to our lives.

Building is better when we have the directions. The result is better if we follow those directions. The job is easier and happier when we do it together rather than alone.

So come, build with me!

Amen.

All The Throws

Can he make all the throws?

When NFL analysts are evaluating quarterbacks coming out of college, that's one of the things they're looking for, one of the questions they ask. An NFL team's passing offense includes a wide variety of plays and routes, but it doesn't do any good to call a particular passing play if your quarterback can't make that particular throw. They want to know: Can he make all the throws?

Can he throw the long ball? Can he throw on the run? Can he get it to the flat with velocity? Does he have arm strength? Accuracy? Touch? It's high praise when an analyst, scout, or coach declares, "He can make all the throws."

A few chapters into Matthew's gospel, we read the account of Jesus calling his first disciples. They were the familiar quartet of fishermen-brothers: Peter and Andrew, James and John. They may not have been a distinguished lot, but they were not questionable characters.

A few chapters further into the gospel, we see Jesus calling another of his inner-circle disciples, and this one was an eye-popper. "He saw a man, called Matthew, sitting in the tax office, and he said to him, 'Follow me!'" Fishermen were not socially, politically, educationally, or religiously distinguished, but they were not objectionable characters. A tax collector, on the other hand, was a scandalous inclusion.

In our day, we may easily miss the significance of the calling of Matthew. First, we are so accustomed to the stories of Jesus reaching out to and including otherwise marginalized people that we may no longer recognize the beauty of it. Second, we hear "tax collector" and think "IRS." It may not be a fond association for us, but it is hardly the sort of offense that Matthew was for the Jews of his day. Third, we have lost touch culturally with the idea of "sinner." Indeed, the very notion of "sin" has largely disappeared from our culture's lexicon, and we certainly do not have a type or category of person that is universally regarded and rejected as "sinner." Accordingly, it is hard for us to appreciate the scandal of what Jesus did.

The Jews of Palestine in Jesus' day were not a free people. They had some generational memory of freedom and independence; their grandparents could remember the days before Palestine was occupied by Rome. But for the present generation, there was resentment and growing unrest as the people chafed under the cruel and oppressive occupation of the Roman forces.

Yes, Rome brought some version of peace, as well as commerce, roads, and a certain sort of safety. But the reality is that the people were easily pushed around and taken advantage of by the soldiers, the local leaders were severely limited in their leadership, and Roman "justice" was often vicious toward those who were not Roman citizens. Rome clearly believed that criminal punishment functioned as a deterrent, and so it was designed to be as severe and inhumane as possible.

Then there were the taxes. Many of the peasants of first-century Palestine merely subsisted. Life was fragile, and they lived precariously on the border of poverty. In that context, then, the burden of Roman taxes was disastrous. While the free citizens of America can at least console themselves with the services and protection that come from their tax dollars, all that the Jews of Jesus' day knew was that they were underwriting their own oppression. It was a bitter pill to swallow, indeed.

The final indignity in the whole system, then, was the individual who served as the tax collector. It wasn't a Roman; it was a Jew. So often, you see, it was one of their own who had betrayed their people and their land in order to conspire with Rome. And why? Probably for no more noble or defensible reason than personal gain — the opportunity to leverage Roman authority in order to line one's own pockets. It was a detestable business, and the tax collectors were detested.

It is worth noting that, in Matthew 21:31, Jesus put tax collectors together with prostitutes. That may have reflected the attitude and paradigm of the culture. Even if there was a widespread recognition that everyone is a sinner, these people were different, maybe worse. There were people, you see, who sinned for a living.

When Jesus called Matthew to follow him, therefore, it was a scandalous choice for Jesus to make. Lest that choice be overlooked as an anomaly or excused as a momentary lapse in judgment, the next thing we know, we see Jesus dining with "many tax-gatherers and sinners." These people had become his companions. This is the unthinkable social club he had chosen for himself.

So much of what passes for charity in our world, you know, is at-arm's-length. I sit in the comfort of my living room as I write my check to support the homeless shelter. It is well-intentioned, to be sure, and better to write the check than not. But will my willingness to help take on other forms, as well? Will it include messy and disturbing interactions? Will it include discomfort for me, and even sacrifice?

I ask these questions not as a cheap guilt trip, but as a recognition of the beauty of Christ. His concern for sinners was not arm's-length. Rather, he came right into their midst, right into their lives. What is writ large in the incarnation itself is played out again and again in hundreds of smaller scenes, including the dinner table in Matthew's house.

But then came the Pharisees.

In our day, our view of the Pharisees is likely a perverted one. We think of them as the bad guys, when in fact they were some of the best people around. They were earnest, orthodox, devout, and in many ways exemplary. But earnestness always has its eccentricities. The half-baked believer isn't likely to go too far in this way or that. It is only the person who is truly passionate and committed that is likely to extrapolate into some extremist misapplication.

The Pharisees honored the law of God. Good for them! But then, in their devotion to the law, they often evolved into legalists.

The Pharisees were committed to purity. Bravo! Purity is an undervalued commodity in our day. Yet in their devotion to being pure, they often became finicky about perceived contamination. That turned into a detached and judgmental posture for their living.

The Pharisees, therefore, would never have sat where Jesus was sitting or dined with the people that Jesus was rubbing elbows with. Theirs was holiness run amok. In their misguided sincerity, they criticized Jesus for what he was doing and how he was doing it.

In response, Jesus said to the Pharisees, "It is not those who are healthy who need a physician, but those who are sick."

His logic was inarguable.

Interestingly, Jesus did not deny the Pharisees' basic paradigm; only their response. He acknowledged the spiritual condition and need of the people with whom he was associating. But it was that very need that necessitated the association.

In our day, we often confuse love with wholesale acceptance. Yet Jesus did not reply to the Pharisees' objection with a defense of the sinners. He didn't say, "You're all wrong about these people and how they live." No, he was candid about the diagnosis. But it was that very diagnosis that led him to behave the way that he did.

The Pharisees' warped sense of holiness chose to identify certain people as sick, and then leave them that way: condemned, abandoned, and uncured. In our often warped sense of love, meanwhile, we hesitate to call anyone sick, lest we seem judgmental. But Jesus, whose holiness was greater than the Pharisees' and whose love is greater than ours, was willing both to make the diagnosis and to bring the cure.

The image of Jesus bringing the cure continues into the next portion of our reading. This time, however, the cure takes a different form. In the episode with Matthew and the other sinners, the "sick" and the "physician" were both metaphors for spiritual realities. Now, however, the sicknesses are very tangible and physical.

First, there is the "synagogue official." We know from other accounts of the episode, in Mark and Luke, that his name was Jairus. He had a young daughter at home. In Matthew's recounting of the story, the girl had just died. Still, this Jairus was confident that Jesus could heal.

This is a remarkable business. In our day, we know better than any previous generation about medical experts and specializations. You may have your primary care physician, and he or she will look you over from head to toe. But if there is a problem, your doctor will very likely refer you to a specialist in heads, or toes, or any part in between.

We are also acquainted with various hospitals and medical centers that have become known for certain specialties. This is where you want to go if you need heart surgery. This is where you take a child with cancer. This is where they are doing groundbreaking work with memory care.

We have all sorts of experts and specializations, yet where do we refer the loved one whose family member has died? Is there a clinic somewhere that takes care of that sort of thing? No, all we know to do — twenty centuries after the time of Jairus — is to call the coroner and the funeral home.

But Jairus called Jesus.

Then, while Jesus was on his way to Jairus' home, the traffic was suddenly stopped. A woman, whom Matthew describes as "suffering from a hemorrhage for twelve years," came to Jesus for healing. This woman's story is a different sort of heartbreaking. We recognize immediately the grief of the father whose daughter has died. But there is a different sort of grief that is represented by this woman. This is the grief that comes with long suffering. This is the grief of being incurable. This is the grief of no longer having the strength or the resources to go on. Yet this woman got it in her mind that "if I only touch his garment, I shall get well."

This, too, was remarkable faith. This woman is so convinced of Jesus' power that she does not even feel the need to get his attention. She does not believe that her healing must be an act of his will, but only the result of the slightest contact with him.

Again, translate the situation to our day. We all know what it is to go to a doctor or a specialist, a clinic or a hospital, an emergency room or urgent care facility, with high hopes that they will be able to fix what isn't right. But who in their right mind expects that merely brushing up against a doctor's lab coat in, say, the hospital elevator will be enough? Who expects to be cured, not by procedure, but by contact? We may fear becoming sick through contact, but no one figures they will become healthy through contact!

This is the outrageous faith of this chronically ill and desperate woman. She didn't throw herself before Jesus, lamenting her condition and begging for his help. She merely reaches out to touch the bottom of his robe.

What possible reason did she have to believe that this would work? After all, Luke reported to us that this woman had spent all she had on doctors, but that no one had been able to heal her. You would think that she would be a person without any hope, at all. Yet, instead, we observe that she has outlandish hope.

Charles Wesley sang, "All my trust on thee is stayed, all my help from thee I bring."[5] Surely this was the posture of the bleeding woman. Her whole trust was placed in Jesus, and all her help came from him.

And came from him it did! The woman was healed in that moment. Then Jesus proceeded down the road to the home where the young girl's lifeless body was surrounded by mourners.

When Jesus arrived at the house, he reassured the grief-stricken people there that the girl was only asleep. Matthew told us that they laughed at him. We recognize the impulse, for it echoes through the centuries. Abraham and Sarah, likewise, laughed at the preposterous promise of God (Genesis 17:17, 18:12). Canaan was the very land of God's promise, yet Joshua and Caleb's contemporaries were unwilling to believe God could give it to them. (Numbers 13:26-33). The royal official scoffed at God's guarantee of abundant provision (2 Kings 7:2). The scene at Jairus' house was neither the first nor the last time that someone has laughed at the Lord.

---

5 Charles Wesley, "Jesus, Lover of My Soul" (1740), UMH #479 (in the public domain).

And why? Why did they laugh at Jesus' word that day? For the same reason human beings always presume to laugh at the Lord: because we think we know better. Sarah knew, you see, that a woman her age couldn't bear children. The Israelites knew that they couldn't defeat the bigger and stronger inhabitants of the land. The friends and neighbors of Jairus knew that the girl was dead.

The pattern in scripture prompts a question for us to consider individually. In what area of life have we thought that we know better than God? In what circumstance are we unwilling to believe his promises? In what relationship or situation do we choose despair rather than hope simply because of what we reckon is impossible?

Jesus put out the scoffers, took the girl by the hand, and raised her to life.

The sample size is a small one — just fourteen verses — yet that is enough to show us the astonishing versatility of Jesus. The one who said that it is not the healthy but the sick who need a physician proved himself to be the consummate physician, the great physician. He brought the cure for those who were spiritually sick, he exuded healing power for those who reach out to him, and he even healed those who were beyond any cure: He raised the dead.

He can make all the throws.

Amen.

Proper 6 (11)
Matthew 9:35-10:8 (9-23)

The People Who Aren't In Church

When I was a young minister, I remember encouraging the members of the congregation I was serving then to invite their friends and neighbors to come to church with them. There was an uncomfortable pause. Then one of the folks said what apparently all of them were thinking: "Everyone we know already goes to church!"

That was the impediment my people had at that time. They couldn't come up with a list of folks to invite to church because everyone they knew was already in church. Not that they were all in our church; but they were in some church.

That was 35 years ago. How things have changed!

My guess is that the folks in the church I am serving today don't have that same problem or impediment. You and I today probably don't have any difficulty creating a long list of people we know who don't go to church, who are not part of any church family. Perhaps what Jesus said in this week's gospel lection will give us some insight into the people who aren't in church.

For much of Jesus' teaching ministry, his audience was no doubt filled with farmers and farming families. Ancient Palestine was an agricultural economy, and since most of Jesus' ministry was a peripatetic ministry in the rural north, he was speaking mostly to folks who lived close to the ground, who lived off the earth. It is unsurprising, therefore, that he so often used agricultural stories and images to reveal spiritual truth.

In keeping with that cultural context, then, he told his followers at this particular juncture that "the harvest" was large. That's good news! But, he said, "the workers" were few.

Those folks immediately understood and appreciated what he was saying. They knew that you had to hire a lot of extra workers at harvest time in order to get it all gathered in time.

When he said that the harvest was big but the workforce was small, they nodded knowingly. They understood.

The picture that he painted was a bit of a mixed bag, you see. On the one hand, there was the vision of the fields. The crops were tall and healthy and ripe as far as the eye could see. Magnificent! A happy sight!

Ah, but when he added the detail that there were not enough workers, suddenly the mood changed. That same sight — the panorama of ripe fields — looked very different. It had the look of lost opportunity. It looked like waste. It looked like trouble and sadness.

You and I recognize that when Jesus spoke of the harvest, he wasn't talking about corn or wheat. Rather, he was talking about a spiritual harvest. We get pictures of that harvest in other parables that Jesus told.

In one story, for example, he portrayed the world as a field — a "field of souls," as one Christian songwriter has called it. The good wheat that grows in the field represented the people who are part of the kingdom of God, while the weeds represented those who belonged to the evil one. The harvest symbolized the final judgment when the wheat and the weeds would be separated.

This is the parable that inspired the Henry Alford hymn that many of us are accustomed to singing at Thanksgiving time. "For the Lord our God shall come," Alford wrote, "and shall take the harvest home; from the field shall in that day all offenses purge away, giving angels charge at last in the fire the tares to case; but the fruitful ears to store in the garner evermore."[6]

In another parable, the world again is a field. This time, however, the "field" is comprised of several different types of soil. The seeds that are sown there represent the word of God. And the different types of soil, then, effectively portray the different ways the people respond — or fail to respond — to God's word.

It is a spiritual harvest: a field of souls. When Jesus spoke of that spiritual harvest, he said that it was a large one. That's very good news, indeed.

6   Henry Alford, "Come, Ye Thankful People, Come" (1844), UMH #694 (in the public domain)

Yet, candidly, the spiritual harvest may not always seem so large to us. There are so many half-full churches. So many churches are struggling for members, straining just to keep their doors open. So many churches are so much smaller than they used to be. We may want to ask, "Lord, if the harvest is so plentiful, where are all the people? If the harvest is so abundant, why aren't there more people in church?"

Happily, Jesus addressed that question and concern. He spoke explicitly about the people who are missing — the people who aren't in church, if you will. But it may not be the people that we think!

We are well acquainted with the statistics and the trends. A large and growing percentage of the population has only vague beliefs about God, little knowledge of his word, and no interest in organized religion. Those people — and there are more and more of them! — are not in church.

But then, why should they be?

The unsaved and the unbelievers, you see — the disinterested, the disaffected, the distracted — they are all precisely where one would expect them to be, perhaps even where they ought to be. They are "out there." After all, where did we expect the harvest to be? It doesn't grow inside the barn!

So the harvest is plentiful, indeed: a bumper crop! It is arguably the largest spiritual harvest in American history! But the crop, of course, is outside; it's not inside.

The people who have no interest in God or in church are not actually the people who are missing from church, therefore. Those folks are right where they are supposed to be. They are the field. They are playing their roles just fine.

No, according to Jesus the people who are missing are the workers — the ones who bring in the harvest. "The harvest is plentiful," Jesus said, "but the workers are few!" That is the group that is missing, you see. Those are the people who are not in church.

I don't want that thought to sit for long before I hasten to add that I know it's a foolish thing for me to say.

I have spent my whole life in the church, and so I know very well that it is ridiculous — and hurtful — to say that the people who aren't in church are the workers. The church I have known throughout my lifetime has so many workers, and such hard workers. I have seen them in kitchens and in gardens, in Sunday school rooms and in bake sales. I have seen them teaching Vacation Bible School, folding bulletins, and stuffing envelopes. I have seen them serving as ushers, as liturgists, and as members of the choir. I have seen them visiting hospitals and singing in nursing homes.

The church I have known throughout my lifetime has so many workers, and such hard workers. I depend on them, I love them, and I admire them. Almost everything that goes on in the church depends upon its marvelously, wonderfully good workers. Most churches would cease to exist if it weren't for all the workers.

Ah, but here is the concern raised by Jesus' teaching. For all of the hard work that we do in the church, we may from time to time forget that the real work we've been commanded to do is not in the church. It's in the field!

What if, one October day, you tell your children to go out and rake the yard, but they chose instead to stay inside and clean their rooms? What if, one January morning, you send them out to shovel the snow, but they stay inside and wash the windows? They're not being bad. On the other hand, neither are they obeying.

Imagine that, at the end of the day, we will all stand before the owner of the field, and he will ask us, "Did you finish the work? Did you bring in that marvelous harvest, as I told you to?"

What will we say? How will we answer him?

"No, sir, we didn't actually bring in much of a harvest, but we sure did make the barn look pretty! Have you seen it? Best barn in town!"

He will ask, "Did you finish the work? Did you bring in that bumper crop, like I told you to?"

What will we say? How will we answer? "No, we didn't actually follow your instructions, but we were very regular about getting together to listen to them!"

He will ask, "Did you finish the work? Did you bring in the harvest right outside your door?"

What will we say? "No, we didn't actually do much work in the field, but we sure had a good time having meetings and fellowship together in the silo."

The workers — according to Jesus — the workers are the folks who are missing. The workers are the people who aren't in church.

Talk of "workers" can be misleading. We mustn't give or get the wrong impression. You and I are not saved by our works. What we report to the owner of the field at the end of the day is not the basis for our relationship with him. We are saved by his grace, not by our works.

Ah, but there is this critical caveat. I may not be saved by my works, but other people are. Other people may be saved by your work and by mine. That is precisely the issue with the field of souls.

Or, to better understand the principle, we might observe how we have been saved by other people's work. Roll the credits of your life, and see how many, many people contribute to your testimony. It is because of that Sunday school teacher, that pastor, that parent, that youth worker; it is because of that college roommate, that author, that grandparent; it is because of those earnest folks working in the spiritual fields that you and I know the Lord today. We are not saved by our own works, but make no mistake that our salvation is owing to the work of many other people!

I wonder, therefore, if we might do well to rethink the borders and boundaries of our world. Perhaps you and I go through our days thinking, "Here is the place where we live, and there is the place where we shop. Here is the place where we work, and there is the place where we vacation," and so on. But it may be that, in the big picture, all of those borders and boundaries and distinctions are irrelevant.

Perhaps, instead, wherever you and I go, we are always in the same place. Whether we are at work or at school, whether shopping or on vacation, we are always moving about in the field of souls. Wherever we are going and whatever we are doing, we are in his field, and he urges us to work his field. Because the harvest is so plentiful, you see!

Walk out the doors of the church — the barn — today, and behold the harvest all around you. Everywhere you go: souls! If those souls are won for Christ — if they are "brought in" — then the field is a very pretty picture. The enormous crop is a happy sight.

Ah, but if the workers aren't there to do the job, then that same sight looks very different. It looks like lost opportunity. It looks like waste. It looks like trouble and sadness.

Make no mistake: the harvest is plentiful. There is nothing wrong with the harvest! Those people are exactly where you would expect them to be, for the harvest doesn't grow in the barn.

Ah, but the workers. Jesus' lament is about the workers. They, ironically, may actually be the people who aren't in church. The workers are few.

Amen.

Sticker Shock

Jesus was no salesman.

In our consumer culture, it is customary for salespeople to emphasize the benefits of a product, while minimizing the price. Indeed, we're all familiar with the phenomenon of "the fine print." And the information contained in the fine print is usually the sort of thing that a salesperson doesn't want to talk about — restrictions, limitations, exclusions, additional taxes and fees, and such.

If *Consumer Reports* says that this is the top ranked product of its kind, that information isn't relegated to the fine print. If the product has all sorts of hidden costs, that's not the sort of information that gets printed on the billboard. It is customary, you see, for salespeople to emphasize the benefits of a product, while minimizing the price.

Jesus was no salesman.

Salespeople know what our customer mentality is. We want to get as much product or service as possible for as low a price as possible. But Jesus turned the tables on the traditional sales pitch. Rather than minimizing the cost, he emphasized it. He seemed to want to make quite certain that you and I knew exactly what we were getting into when we decide to follow him.

Jesus was no salesman, and we can be glad for that.

After all, have you ever felt buyer's remorse? Do you know the experience of realizing, after the fact, that you've been sold a bill of goods? Have you been snookered by some smooth-talking sales representative along the way, and you're saddled with a product, a property, or a policy that you regret or that has become a burden?

That will never happen with Jesus Christ. There is no fine print with him. He lays it all out plainly before us so that we know precisely what are the costs associated with discipleship.

In the tenth chapter of Matthew's gospel, we read that Jesus sent out his disciples to embark on a mission in the towns and villages of Israel. Interestingly, we aren't given any specific details of their mission — where they went, what they said, whom they encountered, or the like. What we are given in some detail, however, is Jesus' instructions to them before they went.

That's a great treasure for us, of course. If we were furnished with lengthy accounts of the disciples' activities, that might be of historical interest, but it would feel far removed from us. Conversely, to know what Jesus said to his followers before sending them out is of great personal interest to us. To the extent that we understand ourselves to be his followers today, and to the extent that we understand ourselves to be sent by him, as well, we may regard these instructions as being addressed to us, just as they were to Peter, Andrew, and the rest of the crew.

He tells his followers that "a disciple is not above his teacher." That's an easy teaching; we never thought that we were above him. Rather, he said, "It is enough for the disciple that he become as his teacher." Indeed! Could we entertain any higher aspiration than to be like him?

Then Jesus turned to the implications of his remarks. "If they have called the head of the house Beelzebul," he observed, "how much more the members of his household!" The remark alludes to the sort of misunderstandings and false accusations leveled against Jesus. His point was that, inasmuch as a disciple aspires to be like his or her teacher, the disciple should expect to be treated the same way the teacher was treated.

"If the world hates you," Jesus told his disciples at the Last Supper, "keep in mind that it hated me first" (John 15:18 NIV). You see the logic. If we follow him, we will aim to be like him. And if we aim to be like him, we may expect to be treated like him.

So let us consider how he was treated.

Here, again, we see that Jesus is the anti-salesman. If he was going to employ more strategically the principle of his followers experiencing the same things he did, perhaps he would point to the popularity — crowds of people always seeking him out and paying him attention. Perhaps he would highlight the Palm Sunday parade. Perhaps he would point to the acts of great love and devotion that he received along the way from certain people.

But, no, he did not try to entice his followers with promises of comfort or fame. Instead, he chose the unfairness of his own experience, and he made it clear that his followers could expect the same treatment.

Meanwhile, this counterintuitive pattern of circling, highlighting, and emphasizing the price continues later in the passage. "Do not think that I came to bring peace on the earth," He warned: "I did not come to bring peace, but a sword." Would he overthrow Rome? No, but rather he pointed to an unexpected and undesirable conflict for his followers. "I came to set a man against his father, and a daughter against her mother, and a daughter-in-law against her mother-in-law; and a man's enemies will be the members of his household."

Surely it was not his desire to break up families, as though that were the goal of the kingdom of God. No, but it was his sober warning to would-be followers that some love relationships will be the collateral damage of following him. Perhaps that has been part of our own, painful, personal experience. We certainly know that church history is full of such stories — believers who have been ridiculed, ostracized, and even disowned by family members because of their faith in Christ.

For some of us, of course, this choice is unfathomable. Perhaps we ourselves were raised in a Christian home. And perhaps we have, as adults, been blessed with a Christian marriage and the beauty of raising children who know and love the Lord. For such folks, a choice between family and following Jesus is incomprehensible, for family has for us been an integral part of following Jesus. If so, that is a beautiful thing, and surely pleasing to God.

The real point, however, is the price tag and the willingness of the disciple to pay the price. This brings our attention to what many of us might identify as the highest price tag of all. "He who loves father or mother more than me is not worthy of me,"

Jesus said, "and he who loves son or daughter more than me is not worthy of me."

On first hearing, this teaching of Jesus can feel very harsh. In reality, it is the most natural thing in the world. Indeed, it should come as no surprise to us whatever.

When the Bible tells us the story of Adam and Eve, it also introduces us to marriage in a more general way. And along the way, the narrator provides this insight: "For this reason a man shall leave his father and his mother, and be joined to his wife; and they shall become one flesh" (Genesis 2:24 NASB). The brief portrait of marriage is beautiful, and it is one that Jesus reiterates during his own ministry (see Mark 10:1-9). Yet the joining also necessitates some leaving.

The Genesis passage suggests a movement, you see. It is a movement toward the spouse, of course. But it is, at the very same time, a movement away from parents. The man in the verse is not just connecting to his wife in a new, profound, and permanent way, he is also disconnecting from his parents.

Is this a tragedy? Do we question the goodness of marriage because of this movement? No, we simply recognize that this is always the nature of love and commitment. To love someone and to commit yourself to them will always mean leaving some things behind. I cannot prize anyone or anything in my life as precious without it requiring me in some ways or times to subordinate other things to it or sacrifice other things for it.

The man and the woman who marry are choosing to leave all sorts of specified and unspecified things behind in order to be together. In some traditional wedding vows, we ask the man and the woman to promise that they will, "forsaking all others, keep thee only unto him/her." Forsaking all others. To love is to leave.

Then they become parents, and the principle is recapitulated at yet another level. They will do more sacrificing, more disconnecting, and more leaving behind for the sake of love. The teaching of Jesus is not harsh, you see: it merely reaffirms what we already know and experience in our other love relationships.

This, then, makes the teaching quite the opposite of harsh. It is, rather, a beautiful teaching, for it is a teaching about love. Indeed, the greatest love of all.

Earlier, we used the image of a price tag. Price tags are a way of measuring and reflecting value. Who can argue with the price tag of discipleship when we consider the value involved? The disciple is the person who follows Jesus — the person who lives henceforth their life with him. What is more valuable than him?

This is the calculation made by the man who stumbled across treasure buried in a field (Matthew 13:44). He reckoned that it was better to sell everything he had in order to afford the field, for he knew that the treasure buried there was more valuable than all that he sold to gain it. Likewise, this was the calculation made by the pearl merchant (Matthew 13:45-46). He knew that the pearl of great price was more valuable than all of the assets he liquidated in order to purchase it.

At another level, this was the testimony of the Apostle Paul, as well. After reciting for the Philippians a summary of his accomplishments and the things of which he had been most proud, Paul wrote, "But whatever things were gain to me, these things I have counted as loss because of Christ. More than that, I count all things to be loss in view of the surpassing value of knowing Christ Jesus my Lord, for whom I have suffered the loss of all things, and count them mere rubbish, so that I may gain Christ" (Philippians 3:7-8 NASB).

"Surpassing value," you see. The price tag is a reflection of the value. All his true followers through the ages have concluded, with Paul, that Jesus is worth the price, for he is of "surpassing value." Paul's statement that he had suffered the loss of all things — and willingly so — "so that (he) may gain Christ" was the embodiment of what Jesus was teaching in Matthew 10.

Over against the joyful testimony of the apostle, meanwhile, is the sad example of the rich young man (Matthew 19:16-26). He could have made the same calculation of those we have just recalled. He could have traded in all that he had in order to gain Christ. Jesus offered him that chance when he said, "If you want to be complete, go and sell your possessions and give to the poor, and you will have treasure in heaven; and come, follow me" (verse 21). But this person didn't see clearly the relative value of things. Luke poignantly reported, that the man "became very sad, for he was extremely wealthy" (Luke 18:23 NASB).

We have suggested that Jesus was not a typical salesman, for rather than hiding the price tag, he highlighted it. Rather than relegating the costs to the fine print, he made them the headline. But perhaps that isn't such folly, after all. Perhaps to emphasize the price tag is to affirm the value.

If what the field-buyer, the pearl merchant, and the apostle all concluded was true, then to highlight the price was actually a selling point. When we are seeing clearly, we recognize that we gain more than we lose. The value of what we receive surpasses the value of what we leave behind.

Jesus was no typical salesman — that is for sure. The typical salesman would try to pad the profit margin and try to get more for the product than it was actually worth. But not Jesus. This was all generosity and grace. He offered us much more than we could ever have apart from him.

Amen.

Emissaries Of The King

"King Hanun, there are emissaries here to see you."

"Emissaries? From where? From whom?"

"From Israel, your majesty. King David sent them here to express his condolences over the recent death of your father."

"How very kind! They are most welcome in my kingdom! Show them in."

"No, wait," an advisor to the king interrupted. "These men are not here to express condolences. That is only a ruse. David has actually sent them here as spies."

"Do you think so?"

"I'm sure of it."

"Then what do you recommend we do?"

"Well, we certainly should not welcome them so openly or so warmly."

"Indeed!"

"No, let us instead teach them a lesson. We will prove to David and to them that they didn't fool us."

"Yes!"

"We needn't harm them. We should simply show them that we see through their plan. We should embarrass them, and then send them home."

"Yes, good advice. We will mistreat these spies, and then send them back where they came from in disgrace."

That is how the conversation may have gone that day in the court of Hanun, king of the Ammonites.

The Ammonites were nearby neighbors to the Israelites. Hanun ruled part of the land that was east of the Jordan River, while King David reigned over most of the land west of the Jordan. As the former king of the Ammonites had died and a new king had ascended to the throne, the question was what sort of neighbors the Israelites and Ammonites would be to one another. David was trying to be a good neighbor. Hanun's advisors didn't buy it.

What happened next was not violent, but it was humiliating. The emissaries who had been sent by David had both half their beards and half their robes cut off. The shaving of the beard was a kind of public emasculation in terms of ancient Israelite culture. Their robes were also cut off somewhere around their hips, leaving them exposed and embarrassed for at least as long as it took them to find alternate coverings for themselves.

Eventually, of course, the news of this reached King David, and you might imagine what happened next. War. David mobilized his armies to attack the Ammonites. The Ammonites, in response, not only marshalled their own forces, but also hired mercenary troops from elsewhere. It was to no avail, however. David's forces soundly defeated the armies amassed by foolish King Hanun of Ammon.

The whole miserable business could have been avoided, of course. The king of Israel had made a genuine gesture of kindness and friendship. He had taken the initiative to send messengers with a word of comfort and compassion. If only Hanun had received it as such. If only he had recognized David's heart and motive.

Instead, however, Hanun made a terrible miscalculation. He distrusted King David and doubted his motives. Rather than receiving the emissaries in the spirit in which they were sent, Hanun treated them as enemies. In the process, Hanun made himself an enemy of King David.

This was a terrible miscalculation by Hanun. The fact is that David had become the strongest ruler in the region at that time. For the preceding generations of Israel's time in the land of Canaan, they had often been bullied and belittled by the neighboring nations. At various times, the Canaanites, the Midianites, the Moabites, and the Ammonites had all lorded it over the Israelites. And, most recently, the Philistines had been the biggest bully in Israel's neighborhood. Indeed, David's predecessor, King Saul, had been killed in battle by the Philistines.

But David's regime turned the tide. He was an effective military leader, he had competent officers and fighting men serving under him, and the Lord prospered his reign. And so, one border at a time, Israel became more and more secure. By the time of this episode with Hanun, Israel was well on its way to being the major power in the region.

Hanun could have been David's friend. The Ammonites could have been at peace with Israel. But, instead, there was enmity and warfare. And it all started with the mistreatment of King David's messengers.

The Old Testament world had a strong sense for the importance of agency, you see. The agent represented someone else — someone of more importance or power or influence. The agent might be a steward of a master, a messenger from some lord, an ambassador from a king.

Biblical scholars say that the servants of powerful citizens or rulers actually enjoyed a higher status than some free men did. The agent, you see, carried the authority of the one he served. The servant came in the name of the one who sent him. That servant, the agent, was accorded the respect that was due to the master, the lord, or the king that he represented.

To show respect to the emissary, therefore, was to show respect to the king who sent him. To disrespect the one who was sent, on the other hand, was to dishonor the sender. It was a vicarious relationship. By mistreating David's representatives, Hanun had mistreated David.

This principle of agency, which is so poignantly played out in the Old Testament story of Hanun, becomes more profound when we turn to the New Testament.

When Saul of Tarsus was knocked to the ground on the road to Damascus, you recall, he heard a voice, saying, "Saul, Saul, why are you persecuting me?" (Acts 9:4 NASB). Disoriented, and blinded by the light, Saul asked, "Who art thou, Lord?" And the response came back: "I am Jesus whom you are persecuting" (Acts 9:5 NASB).

That is likely a familiar story to us, but stop to place it — that event, that conversation — on the timeline of the New Testament.

Acts 9 came after Jesus' earthly ministry, after the crucifixion, after the resurrection, and after the ascension. Indeed, this episode began with the report that Saul was "still breathing threats and murder against the disciples of the Lord... (and) if he found any belonging to the Way, both men and women, he might bring them bound to Jerusalem" (Acts 9:1-2 NASB). In other words, Jesus was no longer physically present on earth. It was Jesus' followers that Saul was persecuting. Yet Jesus came and said to him, "Why are you persecuting me?"

It is the principle of agency writ large, you see. The followers of Jesus were his emissaries. How Paul treated them was how he was treating the one they represented, the one who had sent them.

Against this backdrop, then, we are well positioned to understand the dramatic teaching of Jesus in this week's gospel lection.

In Matthew 10, Jesus was sending out his disciples on a mission. It is, we gather, a sort of short-term mission. They do not, after all, say a final goodbye to Jesus or to one another at this point. Rather, it seems that Jesus was sending them ahead of himself to the places he himself would eventually go. We don't know many of the details of how the mission itself unfolded — times, places, results — but we are privy to Jesus' instructions, and that is a treasure. And a part of that treasure is the profound principle of agency that Jesus explained to his followers.

"He who receives you," Jesus told his disciples, "receives me." They are his agents, you see. They represent him. How they are treated, therefore, is a vicarious treatment of Jesus himself.

Our word "vicarious" is derived directly from Latin. Interestingly, the underlying Latin word meant "substitute." The disciples of Jesus, then, are sent out as his substitute. That is a heady assignment for them, and it carried dramatic implications for those who received or rejected them.

But Jesus went a step further. Not only did he say that to receive his disciples was to receive him, there was yet another layer. "He who receives me receives him who sent me."

We are reminded that, following his resurrection, Jesus said to his followers, "Just as the Father has sent me, I also send you." (John 20:21 NASB). Our mission, therefore, does not begin with us. Rather, we trace our mission in this world back to God the Father. For he sent his son into this world, and his son has now also sent us. We serve, therefore, as the very highest form of emissary. We are royal messengers, and then some.

When I was a young man in the ministry, it was commonplace for churches to have an "Evangelism Committee." Evangelism, in its biblical sense, means the proclamation of the good news about Jesus. Yet, so often in my experience, the agenda of these evangelism committees was devoted mostly to advertising and church growth. Somewhere along the way, it seems that we got confused about the nature of our mission.

The followers of Jesus are not sent by the church in order to help the church. No, we are sent by God in order to help the world. He so loved the world, after all, that he gave his son. Now his son has sent us.

How did the world respond to Christ's emissaries?

As in Hanun's day, there was whispering and cynicism, misunderstanding and opposition. It was a world that, in so many ways, mobilized to fight against the God who sent his son in love. It was a world that chose often to ridicule and oppose those who come in the son's name.

Perhaps you have seen along the way one of the famous portraits of Jesus weeping over Jerusalem. In that poignant scene, Jesus lamented over the city, saying, "O Jerusalem, Jerusalem, who kills the prophets and stones those who are sent to her! How often I wanted to gather your children together, the way a hen gathers her chicks under her wings, and you were unwilling. Behold, your house is being left to you desolate!" (Matthew 23:37-38 NASB).

He said that Jerusalem "kills the prophets and stones those who are sent to her." God had sent his messengers to Jerusalem, you see. But rather than welcoming the kind initiative of God, Jerusalem mistreated his messengers.

Destruction came upon Jerusalem after they had rejected God's messengers — first the Old Testament prophets, then Jesus himself and his apostles. A generation after Jesus' earthly ministry, Jerusalem was destroyed by the Romans. While historians pointed to political and military factors, the New Testament student saw a different narrative: Jerusalem had rejected the messengers sent to it by God, and the judgment came.

This is reminiscent, you see, of what happened to Hanun. He had misunderstood the emissaries sent by King David. Because he misunderstood them, he mistreated them. And because he mistreated them, he was attacked and defeated by David. It is a sobering business, indeed.

That is the unhappy flipside of the principle. Remember, after all, that David did not send his emissaries as enemies, but as an extension of his friendship and kindness. So, too, with God — and even more profoundly so with God!

That kindness is reflected in what Jesus told his disciples as he sent them out. "He who receives a prophet in the name of a prophet shall receive a prophet's reward," Jesus explained. "and he who receives a righteous man in the name of a righteous man shall receive a righteous man's reward."

It's an astonishing measure of the grace of God that those who merely receive God's faithful servants should be rewarded as God's faithful servants. Remarkable. But such is the generosity of the one who said to the dying thief, "Today you will be with me in paradise." Such is the generosity of the one who killed the fatted calf for the son who had squandered his wealth. Such is the generosity of the one who pays the servants hired last as much as those who had worked all day. This is a God so eager to bless that he requires very little excuse, it seems, to do so!

The coming of Christ is the ultimate kindness of the ultimate king. If only his messengers would understand their high calling and privileged assignment. If only the world to which we are sent would recognize good news as good news. If only they would receive God's kindness as kindness. And if only all people would respond in gratitude to the gracious initiative of the King!

Amen.

Proper 9 (14)
Matthew 11:16-19, 25-30

The Guest List

Some invitations are open invitations. Other invitations are more narrow, more targeted — they have names on them. The open invitation says, "Everyone is invited!" The targeted invitation says, "This particular set of people is invited."

We hear this week an invitation that came from Jesus. At first blush, we may think of it as an open invitation, for it seems to have that quality to it. In fact, however, it was an invitation of the more targeted variety.

Jesus said, "Come to me, all who are weary and heavy-laden."

That has the feel of an open invitation inasmuch as we sense that no one would be turned away. Seventeen hundred years ago, Cyril of Alexandria offered an interesting insight into the folks who were weary and the ones who were heavy-laden. "Jesus called everyone, not only the people of Israel," he wrote. "As the maker and Lord of all, he spoke to the weary Jews who did not have the strength to bear the yoke of the law. He spoke to idolaters heavy laden and oppressed by the devil and weighted down by the multitude of their sins."[7]

Jesus' words have the feel of an open invitation, yet his invitation actually featured a very specified guest list. If you are weary, then this invitation is for you. If you are heavy-laden, then this invitation is for you. "Weary and heavy-laden" are the names on this envelope. If that means you, then perhaps today is the time for your RSVP.

The Apostle Paul also had a word to the weary. "Let us not lose heart in doing good," he wrote to the Christians in Galatia, "for in due time we shall reap if we do not grow weary" (Galatians 6:9 NASB). Interestingly, other English translations employ

7   *Ancient Christian Devotional: A Year of Weekly Readings,* ed. Thomas Oden (Downers Grove, IL: IVP Books, 2007), 163-164.

the word "weary" differently, which gives us insight into both the word and the experience. For example, the NIV renders that same verse: "Let us not become weary in doing good, for at the proper time we will reap a harvest if we do not give up" (Galatians 6:9 NIV). Between these two translations, then, "weary" is equated with "losing heart" and "giving up."

Weariness, in my experience and observation, is often a by-product of discouragement. When people get discouraged, they typically get discouraged about doing something. The people of Moses' day, for example, got discouraged about crossing over into the promised land. The people of Ezra's day got discouraged about reconstructing the temple. The people of Nehemiah's day got discouraged about rebuilding the walls. Discouragement breeds weariness, and together they can keep us from doing good. They make us want to give up, to quit.

It is possible, certainly, to become weary of doing bad, and that often marks a great turning point for an individual. When a person grows weary of their sin and selfishness, of their destructive habit, or their empty pleasures, then they have become weary of doing bad. They want something new — indeed, they want to *be* new — and that lays the beautiful groundwork for repentance and redemption.

Paul's concern, though, was that the people in his audience might become weary of doing good, and we recognize that is a common experience. I think it is easy, for example, for a parent to become weary in doing good. The parent invests so much physical and emotional energy in trying to do what is best for the child. All the providing, all the arranging, all the protecting, all the guiding, all the sacrificing — and yet, on any given day — or perhaps even for long stretches of months or years — the parent may be tempted to wonder, "What's the point?" The child does not seem to listen, to remember, to respond, to appreciate. Indeed, perhaps the child instead resists and resents. The parent lovingly tries to do what's best, but it turns into a battle, which is about as far as it can be from the parent's perfect picture.

I can almost hear Paul saying to that parent, "You're doing good — don't lose heart! Don't give up!"

I think, too, of the husband or wife who is going it alone in their marriage. They are the only one investing in the relationship. They are the only one trying to make things better. It's a tiring thing to be married alone! And it is easy to lose heart and want to give up. But I can almost hear Paul saying to that husband and wife, "You are doing well. Let us not become weary in doing well!"

The employee who has been working so hard and so faithfully, but without much sense of recognition or reward. The faithful person on their knees who has been praying so hard and so long about a matter, but their prayers have not yet been answered. The earnest witness who has been trying to share their faith with a friend, a co-worker, a loved one, but has only met with disinterest, or resistance, or even antagonism. It's easy to grow weary in doing well.

When we struggle and grow weary, we want to give up. This is a fundamental byproduct of weariness: we want to quit. In our day, the phenomenon often occurs under the label "burnout." It's not that we don't believe in the importance of what we were trying to do. It's just the overwhelming sense of futility in what we were trying to do! We have lost heart for whatever the good was that we were doing, and we want to throw in the towel.

Paul said, "Don't do it!" He used an agricultural image to make his exhortation persuasive. "At the proper time," he assures us, "we will reap a harvest if we do not give up."

The farmer, after all, invests an enormous amount of labor without seeing any immediate results. We all understand that, though; we know better than to expect a harvest the day after we plant. Yet what we take for granted in the world of agriculture we seem to forget in other areas of life. Perhaps it's because the "season" is less certain, less predictable, in some of the other arenas where we have been working so hard. But Paul seems willing to take the cause-and-eventual-effect world of the farmer and apply it to our other experiences of doing good.

Jesus, too, employed agricultural imagery in his word to weary people. In his case, he pointed to the work animals that would have been so familiar to the people of his time and place. Specifically, he employed the image of a yoke.

A yoke, you recall, was that heavy piece of wooden equipment that went across the backs of two animals, harnessing them together, and attaching them to the plow they were to pull. A yoke went on the back and shoulders. A yoke was designed to make an animal work. Was this Jesus' relief for those who were weary? Was this Jesus' respite for those who were heavy-laden?

Wouldn't it have been better for him to offer us a mattress or a footrest rather than a yoke? That seems an offer better-suited to those who are weary. Yet while the image of a mattress may be more appealing, it is less realistic.

After all, you still have to face whatever the challenges are in your life today. You still have to undertake the responsibilities that are yours to do. The field — whatever it may be for me or for you — the field still has to be plowed. Jesus' invitation was not about exchanging a yoke for a mattress, but rather about exchanging one yoke for another. Specifically, the invitation was to exchange our current yoke for his yoke. And that meant two things.

First, it meant that a person may have been weary and heavy-laden because they were serving the wrong lord. If so, to take Jesus' yoke — to serve him, instead — was the key to finding rest for their souls. They still have to plow the field, but they did what they did for the Lord Jesus, and that labor of love was lighter indeed than the other lords they may have been trying to serve.

We human beings serve a lot of lords, after all. We don't naturally think in those terms, for we fancy ourselves free people. But when we stop to reflect on what drives us — ambition, appetites, money, pleasing other people, status, being appreciated, being recognized, and on and on — we realize that we serve lords which can make for long, cruel, exhausting, and unfulfilling days.

Then Jesus came along and said, "Take my yoke! Keep living your life, with all of its responsibilities, but stop living it for those lesser, oppressive lords. Do it all for me, instead. Do all that you do for the one who knows you better and loves you more than anyone else. Then you will find rest for your soul!"

"The Christian," according to Eugene Peterson, "is a person who recognizes that our real problem is not in achieving freedom but in learning service under a better master. The Christian realizes that every relationship that excludes God becomes oppressive. Recognizing and realizing that, we urgently want to live under the mastery of God."[8]

Secondly, there is this truth: The yoke typically harnessed two work animals together. That is why, incidentally, the Apostle Paul used the image of a "yoke" when writing about marriage. The yoke suggested two who are connected. It suggested two who are moving forward together; two who are sharing the same burden, direction, purpose, and work.

When Jesus said, therefore, that we should take his yoke on ourselves, perhaps he was inviting us to something additional. Not only are we invited to be under his yoke as our Lord, but we are also invited to be yoked together with him as a companion. If so, then this is surely why we find that his yoke is easy and his burden is light — because he is carrying the load with us!

The prospect is both stunning and beautiful, yet it should not surprise us. All of scripture reverberates with the theme of a God who is — and wants to be — "with" us. He came walking in the garden, he put his tabernacle in the midst of his people's camp, his recurring promise and reassurance to his servants was "I will be with you." He embodied the name Emmanuel, he put on flesh and dwelt among us, Jesus' final promise to his disciples was that he would be with them to the end of the age, and the perfect picture of the New Jerusalem features God dwelling in the midst of his people. Will the one who took our flesh upon himself — indeed, the one who took the cross upon himself — now recoil at carrying our yokes with us?

We return to the truth that Paul used a yoke to capture some of the truth of marriage, and we know that scripture also uses the image of marriage to describe the relationship between God

8   Eugene Peterson, *A Long Obedience in The Same Direction: Discipleship in an Instant Society* (Downers Grove, IL: InterVarsity Press, 2010), 59.

and his people. Of course it stands to reason, then, we are invited to be yoked together with him. What an unspeakable privilege that is: to be connected to him, moving forward together, and sharing the same burden, direction, purpose, and work!

We may initially balk at all of this yoke imagery. We do not necessarily welcome the association of ourselves with beasts of burden, and we are not fond of taking any yoke upon ourselves. But when we are feeling weary and heavy-laden, then we begin to recognize the beauty of the image. We may, indeed, feel that we are weighed down by some yoke (or several). And we long, therefore, for the prospect of exchanging our heavy, chafing, exhausting yokes for one that is easy and light!

Some invitations are open invitations. Other invitations are more narrow, more targeted — they have names on them. This invitation from Jesus had a very specific guest list.

Does his invitation sound like it has your name on it? Do you find that this has been addressed to you?

We hear "weary," and some of us raise our hands, saying, "That's me!" We hear "heavy laden," and some of us raise our hands, saying, "That's me!" And so, when we hear, "Come to me, and I will give you rest," let us come running! Let us take his yoke upon ourselves — the yoke of his lordship and the yoke of his companionship — and discover rest for our souls.

Amen.

Proper 10 (15)
Matthew 13:1-9, 18-23

Making A Case For Gambling

Climb into the mind of the frightened investor. Those in the industry have euphemisms to describe him. They call him "risk averse." They say he has a "low risk tolerance." But the truth about this particular guy is simply that he's frightened. He's scared.

Mind you, he is not miserly or hoarding. Indeed, the wealth that he is so protective of and careful about is not even his own. He is, rather, a servant of a wealthy man — he is a steward — and he has been charged with managing a portion of his master's money.

How much of his master's money? Jesus told us that the master had entrusted to him one talent.

At first blush, that may not sound like much to us. But "talent" was not a unit of currency, like "dollar" or "pound" or "euro." No, a "talent" was typically a unit of measurement for weight. Translated into our terms, a "talent" is usually reckoned to be about 75 pounds.

Well, you do the math. How much would 75 pounds of silver be worth today? That's a significant piece of money. What if it was 75 pounds of gold? That's a fortune!

I expect that different personalities or temperaments show their differences when presented with this sort of opportunity. What would you do if put into the driver's seat of someone else's high-end, high-performance, high-powered sports car? Do you tremble with nervousness and proceed with extreme caution? Or do your eyes light up as you say, "Let's see what this baby can do!"?

By way of analogy, the servant in Jesus' parable was afraid to leave the garage. He was reluctant even to turn on the ignition. He just wanted to slip the protective cover back over the car and tiptoe away.

This frightened servant, according to Jesus, took the wealth that had been entrusted to him and buried it. It was the ancient version of hiding your money under the mattress. This is not just being risk averse; this is being paralyzed by fear.

At the end of Jesus' parable, when the time came to give an account of his stewardship, the servant said for himself what his problem was. "I was afraid" (Matthew 25:25 NASB).

Afraid of what? Was he afraid of money? Was he afraid of power? Was he afraid of responsibility? That's all possible. But I like to think that, above all, he was afraid of failing his master.

At some level, of course, it is a commendable impulse to be careful — even exceedingly careful — with another person's money. He was right not to want to fail his master. The tragic irony, of course, is that in the end he did fail. He failed completely.

I wonder if we've ever had a comparable situation. Perhaps in some circumstance, we failed to do our best because we were afraid of failing. Perhaps, in the fear of swinging and missing, we didn't swing at all.

In a children's version of Jesus' parable, the moral of the story is expressed this way: "The sad but wiser servant knew / he'd made a great mistake: / The master's gold was given / with a task to undertake. / His job was not to hide the gift / but use as best he could; / and if he failed, the master would / no doubt have understood."[9]

I like that poetic moral of the story. I am comfortable with that reassuring expression of the message for children. Yet I take issue with it at one level. I wonder about the prospect of failure.

The children's rendition, you see, operates with essentially the same paradigm as the failed servant. The assumption in both cases is that if you try, you might fail. For the servant, that was enough to make him not try. For the children's version of the story, the fear of failing is ameliorated by the promise of an understanding master. Yet I wonder if the fear of failure is legitimate, at all.

The parable featured, you remember, three different servants who were entrusted with portions of their master's wealth. The

9   Janice Kramer, *Eight Bags of Gold* (St. Louis: Concordia Publishing House, 1964).

other two servants were apparently active in using what has been entrusted to them, and they both came back with a handsome profit. If the sort of failure we fear was a genuine option, then you would expect Jesus to have told the story somewhat differently. Perhaps one of the three servants would try and succeed, a second would try and fail, and the third would not try at all. Yet that is not the paradigm that Jesus presented. The servants who tried, succeeded. The only one that failed was the one that didn't try.

You may be thinking to yourself, "How young, naive, and inexperienced must this guy have been to deny the reality of failure?" I assure you that none of those adjectives applies to me. Indeed, I am well acquainted with failure. I am entirely sympathetic with the third servant who proved to be such a disappointment to his master. I understand his fear.

My encouragement for that third servant — and for myself, and for you, as well — comes from another parable of Jesus. It is the story variously known as the parable of the Sower, the parable of the Seeds, and the parable of the Soils. It is a parable that provides us with an unusual gift, for we have in Matthew 13 not only the story Jesus told but also his interpretation of that story as he explained it in a later conversation with his disciples.

Jesus told the story of a farmer who went out to sow seed in his field. We gather from the start what his method of sewing must have been, for Jesus says that some of the seed fell in this sort of place, while some of the seed fell on a different sort of place, and so on. That does not suggest a picture of someone who was either manually or mechanically planting seeds in the ground. Rather, this was a guy who was scattering seed with his hand. He was, in all likelihood, walking through his field with some sort of a large bag full of seed draped over his shoulder. He dipped his hand in, grabbed a handful of seed, and then swung his arm in a semicircular motion, casting the seed as he walked.

I recognize the gesture. I live in Green Bay, Wisconsin, and I see a fair amount of snow each winter. After clearing the driveway and sidewalks on a snowy morning or evening, it is often my next task to spread some salt. The idea is to help melt (or forestall) any ice where people might walk. I have found that spreading the salt on a cold winter morning is an imprecise activity. Most of it goes on the intended pavement, but not all of it. Some of it invariably flies off onto the piles of snow at the side of the driveway or out into the road.

So it is that the farmer who scattered his seed in Jesus' parable ended up hitting a variety of targets. Some of the seed fell onto the best ground there in the man's field, but not all of it. Instead, according to Jesus, there were other types of soil nearby that also received some of the scattered seed.

First, Jesus mentioned the path. This would not be a paved sidewalk, but it would be the next best thing. I remember a stretch of ground on my college campus where a path had been beaten across the grass between two buildings. There were sidewalks that could have gotten the students there, but the most direct route was right across the lawn. So many students had traipsed and trampled that path that it was completely bald. No grass grew there — nor could any grass grow there — for it was so beaten down by the constant foot traffic.

So it is that the seed that fell along the path did not have much a future. The surface was hard; there was no penetration; and, according to Jesus, birds came and ate the seeds. It's as though the seeds had never been there, at all.

Some other seed, Jesus said, fell onto rocky ground. Anyone who has visited the land of Israel finds it easy to envision this scene in the parable. A tour guide many years ago recounted to our tour group the fable that, after the Lord had created the world, he sent four angels out, each carrying an enormous bag of rocks. The assignment was to spread the rocks to the four corners of the earth. But, as the story goes, one of the angel's bags broke over the land of Israel.

It is rocky territory there. The farmers in Jesus' audience nodded knowingly when he said that some seed fell on rocky soil. This was shallow ground, you see — a little bit of dirt atop the rocky terrain. While the seed that fell there was at least able to penetrate and sprout, the conditions were still not suitable for any crop to truly grow and thrive there. The nascent plans died from lack of depth.

Meanwhile, Jesus said that other seeds scattered by the farmer fell among the thorns. This is, we should note, much more promising soil than the first two. This ground, after all, is clearly good enough that things can grow there. The problem in this case, however, is that there are already things — undesirable and inhospitable things — growing there. The seeds would likely thrive in that soil, if only it had been weeded. But the thorns choked out what might otherwise have grown.

Finally, Jesus said, some of the seed fell on good soil. There it was able to penetrate. There it was able to take root deeply. There it was free to spread out and thrive. There, in that good soil, the farmer enjoyed a superabundant harvest.

At the surface, the story that Jesus told made immediate sense to the folks in his audience. These were largely people who lived close to the land. They recognized the various kinds of places where scattered seed might fall. They equally recognized the varying kinds of results. What did not make immediate sense to Jesus' disciples, however, was the underlying meaning of the parable. Later in the same chapter, we read Jesus' explanation.

The seed, it turns out, represented the message of the kingdom. The different types of soil, therefore, represented the different ways that people responded to that message. In a culture where folks seem eager to classify themselves and others — which sign of the Zodiac, what set of initials in the Myers-Briggs, what number in the Enneagram — Jesus offered us a still more substantive way to classify ourselves. What type of soil am I? What type of soil are you?

We can easily imagine the person who is "hard," like the path. Perhaps they are hard because they have been beaten down by people and by life. For whatever reason, though, they have become difficult to penetrate with the good news. The message bounces off of them, taking no root and making no impact. It's like they never heard it.

We recognize, too, the phenomenon of shallow soil. We know the look of the eager, initial, enthusiastic response, only to see it fade away just as quickly. Something within the individual is drawn to the message, but they do not have the depth to persist and endure.

Then there is the life that is too crowded for God's message to be able to take hold and thrive there. There's a willingness, unlike the hard soil; and there's potential, unlike the shallow soil. But there is simply too much competition. The anonymous Bethlehem innkeeper, who is made infamous each year during reenactments of the Christmas story, is the patron saint of the crowded soil, for he has no room in his inn. And Christ was left out as a consequence of his crowdedness.

The good soil is not described for us, but we infer its characteristics from the soils with which it is juxtaposed. This soil — this heart, this soul — was soft rather than hard; it was deep rather than shallow; and it was available rather than crowded. It is in a soul in which the word and work of God can grow and thrive.

And reproduce!

From the creation story on, we see that reproduction is part of God's design. Trees bearing fruit are central to the story of creation in general and to the Garden of Eden in particular. Fruitfulness characterizes the righteous person (Psalm 1:1-3), the person who is following Jesus (John 15:5-8), and the person who is living under the influence of the Spirit (Galatians 5:22-23). Fruit trees are part of God's perfect creation at the beginning, as well as central to the New Jerusalem at the end. His first commandment to the animals and the humans was that they should "be fruitful and multiply."

Design suggests will, and so we take it to be the will of God that his creation be fruitful, that it reproduce. Specifically, that it reproduce abundantly. The capacity for reproduction that he built into his creation is really quite conspicuous. I saw this statement painted across a truck, which I believe belonged to an orchard: "The question is not how many seeds are in an apple, but how many apples are in a seed." Indeed, it boggles the mind!

All of which brings us back to the nervous investor and the fear of failure.

When we are doing the work of God — like the stewards entrusted with their master's wealth or like the farmer who was sowing God's word — we may be afraid of failing him. The sentiment is commendable, but the fear is unnecessary. Failure is inevitable, you see, but success is even greater.

We don't know whether everything the first and second steward attempted succeeded. We just know that, in the end, they had both doubled their master's money. If they did fail, therefore, their successes dwarfed their failures.

That is the inescapably lovely truth of the parable of the Sower. On the one hand, there is a sobering level of failure built into the story that Jesus told. Three out of four places where the seed fell, after all, amount to nothing. By itself, that fact would be pretty disheartening.

Ah, but behold the fruitfulness of the good soil! Jesus said that the seed that fell on the good soil reproduced thirtyfold, sixtyfold, and even a hundredfold! That is a bumper crop, you see, and it more than compensates for all of the wasted seed and disappointing soil.

You and I may go out into the field — this world — to serve the Lord there boldly and fearlessly. We may scatter the seed with happy abandon. We do so with complete certainty and confidence. On the one hand, we may be certain that much of what we endeavor to do will result in failure. Yet on the other hand, we may be confident that, in the end, the efforts that succeed will eclipse and overwhelm all those failures and disappointments, thirty, sixty, and one-hundredfold.

Happy sowing, and bold investing!

Amen.

Proper 11 (16)
Matthew 13:24-30, 36-43

Hymn Of The Harvest

Henry Alford was a nineteenth-century British clergyman, who was best known in his own day for his outstanding, four-volume commentary on the Greek New Testament. In our day, however, his lasting legacy is a hymn that many churches are accustomed to singing at Thanksgiving time: "Come, Ye Thankful People, Come." We sing it at Thanksgiving time because of its obvious thanksgiving theme, and also because it is full of harvest imagery. But Alford had a bigger harvest in mind than just the gathering of the crops each year "ere the winter storms begin."

In so many cultures, over so many generations, in so many corners of the earth, harvest has been a time of great celebration. It is traditionally a time of feasting and of giving thanks.

Now it seems that much of our twenty-first-century American culture is further removed from the land, and from the cycles of planting and harvest, than perhaps any previous generation of human history. So much of the urban and suburban population of the United States doesn't have any sense for the seasons or the harvest. After all, we are accustomed to being able to buy virtually any item of fresh produce at virtually any time of year in our grocery stores and supermarkets. Unless we are individually related to a farm, we may be a bit removed from some of the beauty of the seasons and from the joy of the harvest.

Likewise, in our day of set wages, signed contracts, and salaries, we may feel a little more removed from the providence of God when it comes to our daily bread. After all, many of us go into a year knowing almost exactly how much money we are going to make during that year.

For generations of agricultural societies throughout history, however, there was no such certainty. There was only hope, along with a strong sense of vulnerability. There were, after all, so many factors that the farmer couldn't control — factors that could ruin him. In so many primitive cultures, the people worshiped gods of fertility and weather, therefore, hoping for the best with their land and their crops.

The ancient people of Israel, by contrast — and later the Christians — affirmed one God: one God who made and who ruled over all of creation. But he was not a capricious, unpredictable god, like so many of the silly deities worshiped by other people. No, this was a God who had bound himself in a covenant-relationship to his people: a God who had made promises, guarantees; a God who had given them his word.

When the people of God gathered in the harvest, therefore, they knew and understood to whom they owed their thanks. The harvest was a celebration of gratitude. But, beyond that, the harvest was a celebration with many layers.

First, the harvest represented the completion of a process — indeed, the culmination of a process. Even if we live far removed from the land, we still have these kinds of celebrations. Graduations, confirmation, the cast party, the awarding of a degree, the ribbon-cutting for a new building, the completion of some major project at work, and the like. We like to celebrate those moments that represent the completion of a process.

In addition, the harvest also represented the reason and the reward for all their labor. Imagine in our day a salaried employee who got paid just once or twice a year. Imagine the giddiness that would come with such an occasional payday! So it was with the harvest: it was the reason and reward for all the farm family's labor for so many months.

Then, too, the harvest also represented the answer to prayers. Because the people understood that so much was out of their control, they understood that they had to rely on God. Their land was as covered by prayer as it was by seed and manure. The beauty and bounty of the harvest, then, was a visible, tangible answer to so many prayers.

The world of the Bible was an agricultural world. Ancient Israel had very few large cities — Jerusalem and Jericho, for example. Mostly, the land was dotted with small towns: towns that were the centers of surrounding acres devoted to farming. These were not big, industrial farms, but small, family farms.

Since the world of the Bible was an agricultural world, we observe that the teachings of Jesus were filled with agricultural images and language. His teachings featured the shepherd with his sheep, the laborer in the vineyard, and the farmer in his field.

But, when Jesus talked farming, he wasn't really just talking about farming. Rather, he was speaking in parables — usually parables of the kingdom. Again and again those parables began with the phrase "the kingdom of God is like…"

He said the kingdom "is like a mustard seed that a man took and planted in his field…" He said that it "is like a landowner, who went out early in the morning to hire laborers for his vineyard…." He said it "is like a sower who went out to sow, and some of the seed fell along the path…"

Time and again, you see, Jesus likened the supernatural and spiritual kingdom of God to the natural and agricultural world of shepherds and farmers, fields and seeds. The hymn writer picked up on that metaphorical use of farm language, singing, "All the world is God's own field, fruit as praise to God we yield." Just as a given farmer has a field from which he hopes to yield a certain crop, so the whole world is like God's field, and he has plans for it. He has hopes for what it will produce.

This is the look, the feel, and the truth of one of the farming parables that Jesus told. "The kingdom of heaven," he said, "is like a man who sowed good seed in his field." And that man, Jesus later explained, represented the Lord himself, the field represented the whole world, and the good seed represented the children of the kingdom of God. The Lord had sown his followers throughout the world, looking for them to mature and grow, to blossom and be fruitful.

"But then," the story ominously continues, "an enemy came and sowed weeds among the wheat, and then went away." That enemy, we are soon told, represents the evil one, the devil. The Lord is not the only one at work here in this field that is the world. No, for the enemy has sown his own influence throughout the Earth, which yields a very different sort of produce.

The older translations, as well as the hymn, speak of the enemy's work as "tares." Many newer translations, meanwhile, simply call them "weeds." But the original Greek word for those unwanted plants is "*zizania*," a word that referred to the poisonous bearded darnel, which the farmers of ancient Palestine knew all too well.

This particular weed was diabolically similar to wheat. It grew to about the same height as wheat, and it was nearly indistinguishable from wheat until both were in the ear. Those dastardly weeds robbed the wheat of some of its resources of soil, water, and sun. But because they were so nearly identical, it wasn't possible simply to go through and weed out the weeds. You had to wait until everything was full grown and then separate the wheat from the weeds. And they did have to be separated, for these particular weeds were mildly poisonous.

The Bible does not speak in a prosaic way about the origins of evil in the world. Instead, scripture uses stories and imagery to convey the truth, including this very effective parable that speaks of a malicious enemy and his characteristic way of working. Secret infiltration — deception — and a product that appeared good at first, but turned out to be poisonous. This enemy hoped to compromise, undermine, or ruin the Lord's crop, the Lord's field.

After all the plants began to grow, the enemy's work became apparent. And, as Jesus told the story, the landowner's hired hands came to him and asked, "What happened? You sowed good seed in your field, so where did all these weeds come from?"

The landowner recognized immediately what had happened. "An enemy has done this," he said. In response, his servants were eager to rectify the problem: "Shall we go and pull up the weeds?" they enthusiastically volunteered. It seemed like a right and reasonable suggestion. The master, however, denied their offer.

This is, you know, a persistent problem for some of the servants of God. Zealous, but ham-handed, we may rush out in premature judgment to try to get rid of whatever or whomever we perceive as "the weeds." The master halted their hasty activity, however, saying, "While you are pulling the weeds, you may root up the wheat with them. Therefore, let both grow together until the harvest."

Until the harvest.

We sometimes wonder about the existence of evil — of pain and suffering, of sin and injustice — in the world. It is, for many folks, their number one impediment to faith. If he is God and he is good, why doesn't he take care of this mess? We are impatient for God to step in and fix it all. "Get rid of the weeds right now," we cry!

But the master took a broader view. There is a process. There is a timing. He bids us to be patient "until the harvest."

The harvest, we discover, represented the final judgment in Jesus' parable. Hear what the master said about the harvest: "At that time," he told his servants, "I will tell the harvesters: First collect the weeds and tie them in bundles to be burned; then gather the wheat and bring it into my barn."

The Thanksgiving hymn writer anticipated that harvest: "For the Lord our God shall come, and shall take the harvest home; from the field shall in that day all offenses purge away, giving angels charge at last in the fire the tares to cast; but the fruitful ears to store in the garner evermore."

It's a picture of the great separation at the end of time. In this case, it is a separating of the weeds from the wheat. We recognize the same theme, however, in the stories of separating the sheep from the goats (Matthew 25:31-46) and separating the good fish from the bad fish (Matthew 13:47-50). In the case of this harvest separation, we observe that the weeds are thrown into the fire.

The "hell" imagery is hard to miss. We may not talk much about hell today, and it is too complex a topic to be relegated to one or two paragraphs in a sermon. For the present, though, suffice it to say that, because of what we know about the justice and mercy of God, we can be assured of these two things. First, that there will not be a single soul in hell that doesn't deserve to be there. And, second, that there will be a great many souls in heaven who don't deserve to be there!

The judgment, therefore — that is to say, the harvest — is the occasion when both God's justice would be fully unveiled and God's mercy will be fully realized. The hymn writer yearned for that day: "Even so, Lord, quickly come," he sings, "bring thy final harvest home; gather thou thy people in, free from sorrow, free from sin, there, forever purified, in thy presence to abide; come, with all thine angels come, raise the glorious harvest home."The Alford hymn is, for many of us, as much a Thanksgiving staple as turkey and stuffing. And the whole season of the year, in keeping with the hymn, can prompt us to think about harvests. But even beyond the season, the holiday, and the hymn, we may let many things prompt us to remember the truths of Jesus' harvest parable. Even something as ordinary as a weed in our garden or yard can be a reminder. When we are reminded, let us remember these things about the harvest. It is the completion of a process. It is the reason and the reward for all the labor, and it is the answer to our prayers!

Amen.

Proper 12 (17)
Matthew 13:31-33, 44-52

Scrapbook Of The Kingdom

For generations, the classic portrait of the American tourist featured a camera hanging around the neck. Cameras are no longer the special equipment of the person on a trip. Rather, it seems that everyone has their camera with them at all times. But those cameras are still essential equipment when we are sightseeing.

When sightseeing, we want to capture memories of our visit and experiences. When the sight we are seeing is especially spectacular, we take multiple pictures of it. With things that are so big or so beautiful, just one picture can't possibly do justice. We have to take multiple views from multiple angles in order to try to do right by the sight.

Who has been to the Grand Canyon or Niagara Falls, Westminster Abbey in London or Notre Dame in Paris, the Great Pyramids of Giza or the Great Wall of China, and taken just one picture there? No one I know! We take multiple pictures in order to try to do justice to the magnificence.

As you read Matthew 13, consider yourself on a sightseeing tour. Our guide was showing us the kingdom of heaven. Yet we discover that a single view couldn't capture it all, and we are given the opportunity to see it from multiple angles. Matthew 13, then, is a kind of sacred scrapbook, as the Lord offers us a series of pictures of the kingdom of heaven.

Two of the pictures in the scrapbook are larger in scale — perhaps they are panorama mode. The first showed the kingdom in terms of four different kinds of soil. The second showed the kingdom in terms of two different kinds of crops. We looked carefully at each of those pictures during the past two weeks.

But in the verses from Matthew 13 selected for this week, we see a quick series of smaller pictures. Each was a picture of the kingdom, yet they are different pictures. Here it looked like a tree. There it looked like leaven. It appeared to be a transaction, and yet, it resembled a fishing net. If you take a look at all the snapshots together, you'll enjoy a wonderfully full picture of the kingdom of heaven.

Let's gather around the kingdom scrapbook together. Join me in looking over the pictures that the Lord was sharing with us. Let us marvel at the scope and the beauty of the kingdom of heaven.

First, we have a picture of a seed — and an exceedingly small seed, at that. If we didn't know better, we might think that such a thing could never amount to much. It looks tiny, vulnerable, and easily dismissed.

But look again! Jesus told us that the tiny seed grows into a substantial tree. Indeed, it is so significant that it becomes home for other creatures! When it was a small seed, it might have been eaten by birds; now they build their nests in its final form — and so it is, again and again!

When the followers of Jesus amounted to a dozen or so nobodies, who were frequently characterized by fear, by doubt, by misunderstanding, and by misplaced priorities, the kingdom didn't look like it would amount to much. When all of the believers could fit into a single room in Jerusalem on the day before Pentecost, the kingdom looked small and easily dismissed. Through the earliest generations of church history, when the first Christians were so severely persecuted and forced underground, the kingdom must have looked terribly fragile and vulnerable.

But look again! See what has become of Christ's kingdom on earth! The followers of Jesus span the globe!

The gospel was written and is proclaimed in hundreds of languages. Every single day, new people from all around the world come to faith in Christ. The church has outlasted every despot that has tried to crush it and every regime that has tried to silence it. How many billions of souls have made their nest in the branches of this kingdom that started so small?

Next, we see a picture of a woman making a loaf of bread. It's an ordinary scene; very homey. Then we see her remove one hand from the kneading. She reaches for a nearby container, takes a pinch of a powdery substance, and works it into the dough. In the end, the whole batch of dough ends up being changed entirely by that tiny bit of leaven that she added into it.

Once again, we are presented with a picture of the kingdom as something tiny, but in this picture the kingdom's role is different. The issue here is not so much that the tiny thing grows into something big, but rather the tiny thing proved to have a big influence. The leaven did not grow into the lump of dough; the leaven changed the lump of dough.

The truth of Jesus' image reverberates through every generation, both personally and societally. When the gospel takes hold in a person's life, the impact is not confined to some small aspect of living. No, the whole loaf is leavened! Likewise when the gospel takes hold in a culture at large. We know the stories of great revivals that have occurred in certain regions or in whole countries. We recall what Luther spawned in sixteenth-century Germany or the impact of the Methodist movement in eighteenth-century England. And, closer to home, we think of the great awakenings in America during the late eighteenth and nineteenth centuries.

What happened during those favored moments in history was no small achievement. It was not easily contained or confined. Instead, reform spread throughout the land. All boats floated higher. The whole loaf was leavened.

Surely the loaf of the whole world was envisioned by the parable. The entire globe longed for the redemption of God's kingdom. But that required a great deal of kneading. It began two millennia ago, and the work continues in this very hour.

Next, we see two pictures that look very much alike. The one features a man who sold everything in order to obtain a certain field. The other features a man who sold everything to obtain a certain pearl. We are reminded of the principle of Pharaoh's two, similar dreams (Genesis 41:32): there is something divinely emphatic about the doubling of the message.

Here the kingdom is represented as a transaction — and a personal transaction, at that. This, then, is a view of the kingdom from a quite different angle than the earlier pictures. One senses that this kingdom picture is less global and more individual.

The characters portrayed in these two, brief, similar parables both make a calculation. They come across a thing — a treasure, a pearl — that they reckoned was worth more than everything else they had. It was a remarkable calculation. But it was still a more remarkable find!

It gives us pause to think of selling everything we have. The thought of total liquidation makes us uneasy. Yet, if we knew for a fact that the treasure we would gain far exceeded all that we would sell, wouldn't it make perfect sense to complete the transaction?

The idea of making an appraisal about the value of the kingdom of God may seem crass, but it is not unbiblical. On the contrary, scripture encourages us to be very calculating in these matters. We remember, for example, that Jesus encouraged his would-be disciples to count the cost (see Luke 14:26-33). Lest the thought of following Jesus be reduced to a sentimental enterprise or a half-hearted resolution, Jesus wants us to run the numbers. He was confident that once we have made the careful calculations — once we have seen clearly the value of everything — we would follow him.

It was a certain sort of calculation, wasn't it, that prompted the prodigal son to return home? "How many of my father's hired hands have more than enough food," the son reasoned, and yet "here I am dying of hunger" (Luke 15:17 HCSB). It may seem crude, yet it makes perfect sense. Once the son had made the comparison, the choice was obvious.

Likewise, the apostle Paul had come personally to the same conclusion as the two men in Jesus' parables. He wrote to the Christians in Philippi about the calculations he had made. "Whatever things were gain to me," he explained, "these things I have counted as loss because of Christ. More than that, I count all things to be loss in view of the surpassing value of knowing Christ Jesus my Lord" (Philippians 3:7-8 NASB).

"The surpassing value." That's the issue of the kingdom, you see, when it comes to the individual and the decisions we are asked to make. The man who stumbled upon the buried treasure and the merchant who discovered the pearl of great price: both recognized "the surpassing value," and they did not delay to give up all they had in order to acquire for themselves what they had found.

The sad contrast to these stories is found in Jesus' encounter with the rich ruler (see Matthew 19:16-22, Mark 10:17-22, Luke 18:18-23). He was not willing to give up everything in order to follow Christ and inherit the kingdom. He did not perceive the surpassing value.

Most of us are naturally sympathetic with the rich ruler. He does not strike us as a bad person. After all, he had followed the commandments, and he demonstrated enough sense and earnestness to pursue Jesus and inquire about the kingdom. And deep inside we fear that we would have made the same decision if we had been presented with his choice. It is essential for us, therefore, to recognize the wisdom of the calculation made by the man who bought the field and the merchant who found the great pearl.

Finally, we see a picture of fishermen who cast a great dragnet into the water. Predictably, the net brought in an assortment of fish, and so the fishermen had to sort through their catch. They pulled the net up onto the beach, and they divided the fish into two categories. The good ones, they kept. The bad ones, they threw away.

This is yet one more angle on the kingdom of God, and Jesus did not leave us uncertain as to the meaning of it. "So it will be at the end of the age," he explained. "The angels shall come forth, and take out the wicked from among the righteous, and will cast them into the furnace of fire; there shall be weeping and gnashing of teeth."

If the mustard seed was a glimpse of the kingdom at the beginning, then the dragnet is a picture of the kingdom toward the end. The mustard seed illustrated the small beginning. The dragnet anticipated universal, eschatological judgment.

If human edifices — like Westminster Abbey or the pyramids — require more than one picture, what will suffice for the kingdom of God? A single picture cannot possibly capture the whole truth about the kingdom. We need multiple angles in order to get a proper sense for the whole thing.

Look at its length, for it stretches all the way from first-century Palestine into eternity! Marvel at its breadth, observing how it applies to the individual yet also encompasses the whole world! And, finally, stand in awe of its height, as it reaches from a manger in a barn all the way to the throne room of the universe! Yes, we will need many pictures in order to capture this sight.

But do not mistake this for a mere tourist attraction. We do not pull up before God's kingdom in a tour bus, clamor out, buy some souvenirs, take some pictures, and move on to the next thing. No, this is a much more profound business, and the pictures that Jesus shows us reveal to us the significance of what we are seeing.

Amen.

Proper 13 (18)
Matthew 14:13-21

Peter And Andrew, James And John, You And Me

I was asked recently which character in scripture I thought I was most like. The question was surprisingly novel for me. I had thought often through the years about which characters I most wanted to become like, but I had not often stopped to think about which ones I am already like.

Since being asked the question I have been reading the Bible with my eyes opened to resemblances. In reading this week's passage from the gospel of Matthew, I find myself a little troubled by the example of the disciples. They look familiar to me.

The disciples of Jesus should be natural allies for us in the text. They are, after all, the people who heard Jesus' call. They were following. They were learning. They were believing. In short, they were very much like you and me.

They were also faltering, which serves to make them familiar to us, as well.

It's important that we keep the disciples from becoming either stained glass windows, on the one hand, or caricatures, on the other. The one risk is that we will so canonize them that they seem far off, and we can no longer relate to them. The other risk is that we will so exaggerate their foibles and failures that we no longer recognize ourselves in them and them in us.

You remember that James said, "Elijah was a man with a nature like ours" (James 5:17 NASB). Well, if Elijah, then so too Peter and Andrew. So, too, James and John. So, too, Mary, Joanna, and Susanna. So, too, Matthew, Philip, Judas, and all the rest of them.

Over the course of the gospels' stories, we observe that the disciples are truly mixed bags. They demonstrate the faith necessary to leave all kinds of things behind in order to follow Jesus, and yet Jesus chided them on multiple occasions for their little faith in the face of storms or troubles or needs. They pledged to follow Jesus to the death (Matthew 26:35), but a few hours later they all ran away (Matthew 26:56). Peter was commended in one moment for being uniquely privy to the things of God (Matthew 16:17), and then scolded in the next moment for being like Satan (Matthew 16:23). Even after the resurrection, we see that they were a mixed lot in the presence of the risen Christ: "When they saw him, they worshiped him; but some doubted" (Matthew 28:17 NIV).

I read the gospels, and I see that the disciples are uneven in their faith, unreliable in their devotion, and inconsistent in their understanding. But I don't hold that against them. I see the same thing in the mirror.

That brings us to the passage at hand.

The story of the feeding of the five-thousand is an important one inasmuch as it holds a rare distinction. This episode is one of only a very small handful of events recorded in all four of the gospels. Matthew, Mark, Luke, and John all told us portions of the story of Jesus, but they didn't tell us exactly the same story. Only Matthew and Luke, for example, told the story of Christmas. Only John told about Jesus turning water into wine. Only Luke recorded the parable of the Good Samaritan. But the material common to all four gospels is fairly small.

Matthew, Mark, Luke, and John all reported the ministry of John the Baptist. They all recorded the events of Holy Week — that is, the things that happened from Palm Sunday through Easter Sunday. And they all included the account of the feeding of the five-thousand.

We read that Jesus was seeking "a lonely place by himself." He had just received the news of the execution of John the Baptist, and he wanted to be alone. But "alone" was hard to come by for Jesus. Instead, he immediately found himself surrounded by crowds of people — "a great multitude," Matthew told us.

We needn't be coy about this, for each one of us has experienced it. We know what it is to have someone waiting for us at exactly the time or place when we hoped to have some solitude, some peace, some rest. It is usually not a malevolent thing. The baby doesn't start crying at that moment on purpose. The seven-year-old doesn't awaken with a bad dream just to spite you. The friend or co-worker doesn't need your ear at that moment just because they want to make life hard on you.

We've all been there. We can imagine, therefore, the reaction we might have had when, upon arriving on the side of the lake where we were going for some time alone, we found "a great multitude" waiting for us. We know the sort of things a person feels in that moment. But Jesus saw clearly, for we read that what he felt was "compassion for them."

The underlying Greek word that we typically translate as "compassion" only appears a dozen times in the New Testament, and eight of those times it is used to describe Jesus. On one other occasion, it is what a desperate father of a sick child asked of Jesus. The remaining three usages were all spoken by Jesus: a word that he used in parables to describe the forgiving master (Matthew 18:27), the Good Samaritan (Luke 10:33), and the father of the prodigal son (Luke 15:20). It is, you see, a significant word, a divine attribute. Wherever it appears, it is followed by some act of kindness, help, rescue, or deliverance.

Matthew did not make it clear just how much time Jesus spent with the multitude. We do know, though, that Jesus "healed their sick." What was summarized in a few words was no doubt the work of many hours. Each healing, after all, probably included a story, an explanation, or a request. Jesus did not wave a plenary magic wand over the crowd and instantaneously heal them. He healed them one at a time, and that takes time.

Then Matthew told us that "when it was evening, the disciples came to him, saying, 'The place is desolate.'" There is an irony in the fact that the place was desolate. That was precisely its original appeal for Jesus. But rather than being a solitary place, it had become a crowded place. As the sun set, it was a place where a hungry crowd could not find any food for themselves. Accordingly, the disciples said to Jesus, "The time is already past; so send the multitudes away, that they may go into the villages and buy food for themselves.'"

Sending the crowd away was no doubt what Jesus probably wanted to do several hours earlier. But he didn't. Now the disciples were urging Jesus to send the crowd away "that they may go into the villages and buy food for themselves." But Jesus said to his disciples, "They do not need to go away; you give them something to eat!"

Jesus was instructing his disciples to do exactly as he had done. He had not sent the crowd away; he stayed and met their needs. The disciples, rather than sending the crowd away, should meet their needs, too.

It was a ridiculous proposal. What group of a dozen people carries on their person enough food to feed a crowd of several thousand people? How wealthy would the disciples have had to be in order to pick up the tab for that size dinner party? In John's account of the miracle, Philip quickly ran the numbers and exclaimed, "It would take more than half a year's wages to buy enough bread for each one to have a bite!" (John 6:7 NIV).

In short, Philip was acknowledging that they didn't have what it would take to meet the needs of the crowd. But while they did not have enough, they did have something. "We have here only five loaves and two fish," they reported to Jesus.

There is no suspense in the story for us because it is familiar. We need to exercise our imaginations in order to place ourselves in the position of those first disciples. They had enough food for perhaps two or three people, which left only 4,997 left to feed (not counting women and children, apparently). Supply was dwarfed by demand.

Jesus said, "Bring them here to me." After having the folks in the crowd sit down to eat, he took the meager supplies, blessed the food, broke the bread, and gave it to the disciples. The disciples, in turn, distributed to the people what Jesus had distributed to them. Somehow, the food kept getting passed along, until "they all ate, and were satisfied." Lest we think that the miracle was in people being satisfied by a mere morsel, we are told that "they picked up what was left over of the broken pieces, twelve full baskets." Just the leftovers exceeded by a factor of ten the amount of food they had when they had begun!

The superabundance of the provision is noteworthy. Surely what we see in this episode resonates with what we see all across the pages of scripture, as well as in nature and in our own experience. Ours is a God of supply that exceeds demand.

The ancient creation story paints a picture of the first humans being literally surrounded by provisions. All these years later, for all of our advances in knowledge and technology, we still have not exhausted the breadth and depths of the wonders of his creation. Furthermore, he built into both plant and animal life an astonishing level of fertility that far exceeds mere survival. He is the God whose freed slaves emerged from the land of their bondage encumbered with treasures. He is the one whose pilgrims find that their sandals do not wear out, even after forty years of wilderness wandering. He is the one whose destination for his people was a land flowing with milk and honey. He is the one who promises a day "when the reaper will be overtaken by the plowman and the planter by the one treading grapes. New wine will drip from the mountains and flow from all the hills" (Amos 9:13 NIV). He is the one who makes our cups overflow (Psalm 23:5), whose emergency wine proves to be the best wine (John 2:10), who gives "a good measure, pressed down, shaken together and running over" (Luke 6:38 NIV), and who is able "to do immeasurably more than all we ask or imagine" (Ephesians 3:20 NIV).

The overabundance of leftovers in this story from Matthew 14 may be miraculous, but it is not unusual. Rather, it is absolutely characteristic of the Lord. It is a reflection of both his power and his love — the goodness of his will and the greatness of his ability.

We recognize the Lord in this episode. What he did for that crowd that day is what he always does. The question is whether we recognize ourselves in the story.

We may identify with the crowd, and that would be good and right. We, like they, do come seeking him out with our needs. He does look upon us with compassion and he does respond to us and our needs with characteristic providence, grace, and generosity. We do well, therefore, to identify ourselves with the crowds.

But perhaps we recognize ourselves, too, in the disciples. His first followers were, after all, our ancestors in the faith, and we follow in their footsteps. Perhaps we recognize the impulse to want to send away needs that seem overwhelming to us. Perhaps we resonate with the feeling that the Lord asks us to do things that are far beyond our capacity and personal resources. For myself, I know that I identify not only with the crowds, but also with the disciples in this episode.

Let me learn the lessons that they learned that day. First, that you and I are to entrust to his hands whatever we have, no matter how inadequate it may seem. Second, that we are the intermediaries of his, but not the source of the power. And, finally, that we serve a God whose will is good, whose power is great, and whose beautiful pattern is cups that overflow and baskets full of leftovers.

Amen.

Proper 14 (19)
Matthew 14:22-33

I'd Rather Have Jesus

One summer night many years ago, our family was making a long, through-the-night drive from Tennessee to Wisconsin. The August weather in Tennessee had been hot and muggy, and those hot and muggy days often gave way to dark and stormy nights. After we had been on the road for about an hour, the kids were asleep in the back seat, and my wife was asleep in the passenger seat next to me. It was very peaceful.

Then I began to see lightning in the distance. It wasn't the jagged individual bolts of lightning that you sometimes see, but rather the kind of full-sky flashes of lightning that suddenly made the night bright and showed the silhouettes of the tall, dark clouds that filled the sky.

As time passed, the lightning became more frequent, like the bubbles in a pot of boiling water — first here, then there, then over there. I drove for more than an hour, just watching the light show off in the distance. Then, seemingly all of a sudden, I was in the midst of it: right in the middle of a terrific electrical storm and downpour of rain.

It was the kind of rain that, no matter how fast the windshield wipers went, the window was a complete blur. I slowed down to about half of the speed limit. Then I slowed some more. Then I slowed to a crawl. Ultimately, I was forced to pull over to the side of the road because there was just no seeing to be able to drive.

As we sat by the side of the road, one crack of thunder was so loud that it awakened my wife. She woke up to discover that we had stopped driving, and were stranded there in the downpour. It was quite a helpless feeling: you couldn't get out of the car because of the storm; but the car couldn't go anywhere either because of the storm.

We just sat, dwarfed by the storm by the side of the road. We sat in the midst of the lightning and thunder, the rain and the wind, just waiting for it to stop.

That story no doubt triggers in your mind your own stories, your own memories of some terrific storms that you've experienced. If this were an informal small group setting, we could spend quite a little time swapping stories together of the storms we have seen. With those storm memories and experiences in mind, we are prepared to think vividly about the story recorded for us in Matthew 14.

It's a storm story. More frightening, though, than a storm in a car, this is the story of a storm in a boat. That's where Jesus' disciples found themselves — in a small boat, out on the Sea of Galilee, at night, in the midst of a terrific storm. They didn't have the luxury of "pulling over" to wait it out. They didn't have the security and shelter of an automobile on solid ground. Instead, they were at the storm's mercy: driven by the hard wind, and tossed randomly by the waves.

Nothing can make you feel quite so small and vulnerable as an angry body of water. You become acutely aware that the water is much bigger, much deeper, and much stronger than you are. The disciples' little boat was in great jeopardy. If it had capsized, they would almost certainly have been lost.

I wonder if, like my night by the side of the road in Tennessee, that night on the Sea of Galilee was completely dark except for the occasional and terrible visibility afforded by the lightning. If so, then perhaps there was a moment when one of the disciples thought he saw something. Perhaps he kept looking in that same direction, waiting for a chance to see it again. He did, and he pointed and cried out, "Look over there! Out on the water!"

Perhaps, then, two or three at a time, the other disciples looked hard, until the lightning gave them a momentary glimpse. A momentary, frightening glimpse of what appeared to be a human being standing out on the water. They strained to see the specter more clearly, wondering if their eyes and the darkness deceived them.

Finally, as they began to panic that the terror of the storm was being trumped by the terror of a ghost, the figure called out to them. It was the voice of Jesus. "Take heart! Don't be afraid! It is I."

He told them not to be afraid. There's no indication, however, that the disciples stopped being afraid. Indeed, it seems that they only stopped being frightened when the storm stopped being frightening, which is so often the way we human beings operate.

This storm story featured two familiar miracles of Jesus: his walking on the water and, shortly after it seems, his calming the storm. Let us set aside for the time being, however, the remarkable things that Jesus did and turn our attention instead, to the remarkable thing that Peter did.

When Jesus first called out to the disciples, Peter responded by saying, "Lord, if it's you, tell me to come out to you on the water." Jesus called, and Peter went.

Every so often while driving about, one sees a bumper sticker that reports what the driver would rather be doing. I'd rather be skiing. I'd rather be sailing. I'd rather be golfing — or some such.

We know the feeling. We know what it is to be in one place when you'd rather be in another place; to be doing one thing when you'd prefer to be doing something else.

I've seen quite a variety of those bumper stickers, but I have yet to find one that reads: I'd rather be in pain, or I'd rather be in danger, or I'd rather be in trouble. I've never seen that kind of bumper sticker. But I have seen that kind of choice.

That is the kind of choice that Peter made when he chose to get out of the boat.

One of the truly lovely parts of pastoring a church is the privilege of officiating at wedding ceremonies. Each time I perform a wedding, I am struck anew by the profound beauty of the occasion, the decision it represents, and the vows that articulate the decision.

At the same time, however, I know that the average young man and woman who repeat those vows have very little idea what they're saying. What pair of 24-year-olds who have been dating for two years, for example, can possibly fathom what forty, fifty, or sixty years of "for better and for worse" actually looks like?

In their enthusiastic love, they make this sober and dramatic commitment. Whatever the future with you may hold, I would rather go through that future with you than without you. For better or for worse.

That is also the nature of the promise we make to Jesus. We commit to follow him for better or for worse. Indeed, the nature of the discovery we make with Jesus is that we'd rather go through worse with him than to go through better without him.

Charles Wesley sang, "Dark and cheerless is the morn unaccompanied by thee."[10] More recently, Wayne Watson sang it this way: "I'd rather walk in the dark with Jesus than to walk in the light on my own. I'd rather go through the valley of the shadows with him than to dance on the mountains alone. I'd rather follow where he leads me than go where none before me have gone. I'd rather walk in the dark with Jesus than to walk in the light on my own."[11]

The avid skier says, "No matter where I am or what I'm doing, I'd rather be skiing." The young man in love says, "No matter what the future holds, I'd rather go through it with her." The disciple says, "Wherever he is, wherever he goes, wherever he leads, I'd rather be there, I'd rather have him."

I think of some young men and women I know — folks I knew when they were teenagers, but who have since grown up, gotten married, and had families of their own. These were kids who grew up in the suburbs, in upper middle class homes — kids who went off and got their college degrees at good schools. They were young men and women who could have made a pretty, safe, comfy life for themselves, but who chose instead to go off into some mission field.

---

10 Charles Wesley, "Christ, Whose Glory Fills the Skies" (UMH #173). (in the public domain)

11 Wayne Watson, "Walk in the Dark," *A Beautiful Place* (Dayspring, 1993). https://genius.com/Wayne-watson-walk-in-the-dark-lyrics

I think of Susan, who has devoted herself to an inner city ministry in a major American city. In spite of the danger, the ugliness, the difficulty, she is there to minister to needs that are way too big and too many. Why? Because that's where he wants her, and she'd rather have Jesus.

I think of Julie and Dan, who left family, homes, and jobs behind here in the States to live a sparse existence, without the creature comforts they grew up with, in order to go off to an African country and run an orphanage. They are caring for little children whose parents are gone for one tragic reason after another. They live miles from civilization — from hospitals, from telephones, from plumbing and electricity — because that's where he has called them, and they'd rather have Jesus.

I think of a family my father told me about years ago. They were a young couple with several small children at the time. They were new members of the church where my dad was the pastor. My dad was aware that they were very generous givers, and he assumed that their generosity reflected the kind of job and salary the man had. When my dad went to visit them in their home one evening, however, he was surprised to discover that they had no living room furniture. They were not generous because they were rich; they were generous because Jesus Christ was first in their lives, and they'd rather have him than furniture or anything else.

And I think of Peter climbing out of the boat.

Do you see the storm that night on the Sea of Galilee? Do you see the boat pitching and tossing, out of control? See how dark it is, except for the occasional flash of lightning that briefly gave the disciples a frightening glimpse of the high waves around them and the ominous clouds above them.

See the men as they cling, desperately, to whatever board or bench or rope or pole that they can. They struggle to stay in the boat, lest the next collision of waves fling them helplessly into the dark tumult of the water.

See them struggling to stay in the boat — that is, up until Peter sees Jesus, and then Peter wants out of the boat!

The boat is their one hope, is it not? The only thing they have to cling to in order to keep them alive. The water is the danger, the enemy, the waiting grave. Who in their right mind gets out of the boat to go onto the water?

Yet when Peter sees Jesus out there on the water, observe the instinct of his heart. Peter would rather get out of the boat and get into the water. And why? Because Jesus is out on the water, and Peter would rather have Jesus.

I'd rather be in the water and in the storm with him than to be in the boat without him.

Left to my own devices, I'd rather have the boat. I'd rather have what safety and security I can make for myself. But if he is in the storm, then let me leave my sorry boat behind, for I'd rather have him.

All through history, this is the nature of the decision that has taken Christian missionaries to foreign lands, that has led Christian businessmen to do the honest thing, that has made Christian teenagers choose purity over popularity, and that has taken Christian martyrs to their death. They'd rather have Jesus.

And one day at a time, this is the kind of decision you and I may make.

I'd rather have Jesus than to be popular — or even understood. I'd rather have Jesus than get even. I'd rather have Jesus than be safe and secure, than cling to this boat, whatever your boat or mine may be.

I don't mean to suggest that the choice to follow Jesus is always a choice for danger or pain or trouble or sacrifice. I do mean to affirm, though, that the choice to follow Jesus is sometimes a choice for danger or pain or trouble or sacrifice.

I don't know what the particular storm may be that will seem so threatening tomorrow. I don't know what the particular boat may be that I will want to cling to tomorrow. But I do know that I may be called to follow in Peter's footsteps — to leave the boat and get into the water; to let go of the boat and cling to Jesus. I know that, in the end, whatever the storm and whatever the boat, I'd rather have Jesus.

Amen.

Portrait Of Prayer

The disciples came to Jesus one day, saying, "Lord, teach us to pray, just as John taught his disciples" (Luke 11:1 NIV).

That's a good request and an excellent impulse. Perhaps many of us recognize that impulse, that desire. It's not that we don't know how to pray, at all. But just as a person who may be something of a writer, singer, or actor has the good sense to want to learn how to perfect their craft from someone more accomplished in the field, so it is with prayer. We sense in someone else a quality of prayer life that exceeds our own experience. If we have the good sense, we will want to learn from them how to do it better.

Who has been that encouraging and challenging example in your life? Perhaps it was a sainted grandparent. Perhaps a pastor or Sunday school class teacher you had along the way. Perhaps an author — Teresa of Avila, Brother Lawrence, Charles Spurgeon, or Thomas Kelly. We have sensed in someone else a facility, an intimacy, a boldness in prayer that shows us that we still have a way to go. We have, in our own way, said (or wanted to say) to that person, "Teach me to pray!"

We understand what the disciples wanted and asked. They were certainly right to want to learn how to pray from Jesus, just as they were right to acknowledge John the Baptist as an instructor in prayer. I doubt, though, that they realized they could learn about prayer from this woman.

Jesus and his disciples were traveling at this time in a region somewhat removed from their usual traffic patterns around the region of Galilee. They had gone to the north and west, up to the region around Tyre and Sidon. This was foreign territory. The woman who taught us how to pray was a foreign woman.

Matthew told us that she was a Canaanite. Canaan, you recall, was the common appellation for the land that the children of Israel were endeavoring to enter and occupy in the days of Joshua. The Canaanites were among the entrenched inhabitants of the land, and therefore were among Israel's historic enemies.

Canaanites are mentioned more than five dozen times in the Old Testament. Almost without exception, the references are negative. Again and again, they are associated with trouble and conflict for the people of Israel. In the New Testament, meanwhile, there is only one person who is identified as a Canaanite, and it is this woman from Matthew 15.

This Canaanite woman is a mother; specifically, a mother whose child is desperately ill. Whatever racial or ethnic prejudices may be harbored by these people against those people, it is a circumstance like this one that should melt away the superficial differences. For this mother from Canaan behaved just as would a mother from Israel — or from anywhere else, for that matter. She was urgent and persistent in seeking help for her child.

We don't know how she had heard of Jesus in the first place, nor how she came to know that he was in the area. What we do know is that she sought him out, and that fact by itself makes her a portrait of prayer. This is a person who has a need, and she brings the need to Jesus. That is faithful prayer.

Inasmuch as you and I also seek him out — inasmuch as we also bring our needs to him — we recognize that we are following in her footsteps. It bears considering, therefore, just what went on in her head and in her heart.

While we don't know what precisely she had heard about Jesus, it was enough to give her some hope that he could help. In addition to the possibility that he would be able to help, she must also have had some inkling that he would be willing to help. Those are separate issues. There are a great many people who are capable, say, of giving me $10,000, but a much smaller number, I suppose, who would be willing to do it.

We look in the mirror. What have we heard about Jesus? What do we know about him? Does what we have heard and what we know inspire us to come to him? Do we come with the confidence that he is able? Do we come with the expectation that he is willing?

This woman stood on the other side of the cross and the empty tomb from us. She had, therefore, so much less to go on than we do. We have so very much more reason to believe that he is willing and to be confident that he is able. We ought certainly to follow in her footsteps. Indeed, we should outpace her!

The woman found Jesus where he and his disciples were walking along, and she cried out to him for help. "Have mercy on me," she pleaded.

Cherished within the Eastern churches of Christianity is the so-called "Jesus Prayer." That simple prayer, which takes slightly different forms in different versions, says, "Lord Jesus Christ, have mercy on me." This is the posture with which we come to him. We do not come claiming our own merit, but pleading his mercy.

The Canaanite woman cried, "Have mercy on me, O Lord, son of David."

"Lord" and "son of David" are both titles. Titles are important, for the titles that we use for a person indicate what we recognize and affirm about that person. It could be something as simple as "professor," "officer," or "doctor." It could be something more personal, like "mommy," "grandpa" or "friend." The titles that this woman used for Jesus were revealing, indeed.

"Lord" was not an exclusively religious word in the New Testament world. In addition to being the title that was used to address or refer to a deity, it was also the common title applied to one in authority over you — a master, a governor, a king, or some such. It may be that this woman was prescient in affirming the divinity of Christ. At a minimum, though, she approached him as a supplicant, recognizing him as one in authority.

Her use of "son of David," meanwhile, was a more remarkable salutation. David was a cherished and heroic figure in Israelite history. David was an important name among the Jews. But there was no reason for David to hold a special place for this Canaanite woman.

Meanwhile, "son of David" carried with it very specific messianic connotations. When Jesus asked the Pharisees, "What do you think about the Christ, whose son is he?" they immediately replied, "The son of David" (Matthew 22:42 NASB). When the hopeful and excited crowds welcomed Jesus into Jerusalem on the occasion we recall as Palm Sunday, they hailed him, crying out, "Hosanna to the son of David" (Matthew 21:9 NASB).

Whether "Lord" was an acknowledgement of Jesus' deity or merely a salutation of human respect and deference, "son of David" was a title with real theological significance. This Canaanite woman was making a genuine affirmation of faith when she called Jesus "son of David." And with that real faith about who he was came real expectations about what he would do.

Then came the expression of need: "Have mercy on me, O Lord, son of David, my daughter is cruelly demon-possessed."

There is no pain like a parent's pain. What wouldn't the parent do in order to bring healing and relief to their tortured child? This poor mother was watching her child be tortured in the worst possible way.

Other stories in the gospels about demon possession give us insight into the mother's characterization of "cruelly." We heard a father report that his son's demon "had often thrown him both into the fire and into the water to destroy him" (Mark 9:22 NASB). We remember what the demons cast out of the Gerasene did to a herd of swine (Mark 5:11-13).

The anecdotal evidence suggests that there is something fundamentally self-destructive about the demonic presence. Given that observation, perhaps we are prompted to suspect that there is more demonic influence pervading our culture than we are prone to admit. Apart from the contemporary scene, we can imagine what that long-ago mother was watching her child suffer.

So it was that Jesus was presented with the heart-breaking plea of a heartbroken mother. Yet, much to our surprise, "He did not answer her a word." This is not what we are accustomed to seeing in the stories of Jesus' earthly ministry. This is not the picture of Jesus that we cherish.

Interestingly, however, the lack of an answer from Jesus did not deter the woman. She must have kept pressing her case, for the disciples came to Jesus saying, "Send her away, for she is shouting after us." That suggests behavior that was continuous, and therefore a nuisance.

Once again, if we recognize that we follow in this woman's footsteps when we bring our needs to Jesus, we are positively challenged by her example. After all, how easily are we deterred when we get no response? How discouraged have we become when we feel that our prayers are met with silence? Do we presume to keep pestering, or do we quit and go home?

It may be that we have other reasons for not persisting in prayer. Perhaps it strikes us as impolite. Perhaps it feels irreverent. Yet Jesus himself taught his followers to press the boundaries of common courtesy with God. We remember his stories of the knocking neighbor (Luke 11:5-8) and the nagging widow (Luke 18:1-8). We think these behaviors are the stuff of bad manners. Jesus, however, held them up as models of exemplary prayer.

This woman was undeterred by the lack of a response from Jesus. She evidently kept after him to the point where the disciples regarded her as a pest and so they prevailed upon Jesus to send her away.

Jesus' response at that moment, then, was a fascinating one. He declared, "I was sent only to the lost sheep of the house of Israel."

What did that answer mean? On the surface, it suggests that Jesus' mission was ethnically narrow. His ministry was meant for the Jews, but this woman was a Gentile. That is the apparent meaning on the surface. Yet what does it mean in its context?

The context, you see, was that the woman was asking him for help and the disciples were asking him to send her away. Within that moment, then, what did his answer mean? What he said would seem to be a discouraging word to her. Yet we are conscious of what he did not say. He does not say, "No." He does not say, "Go away." That is what the disciples were prevailing upon him to say; yet that is not what he said.

Then comes the climactic moment. "She came and began to bow down before him, saying, 'Lord, help me!'" One senses that she had perhaps been trailing up until this moment — following Jesus and his disciples down the road. But perhaps she circled around to the front of the group. Perhaps she put herself in the way. Her position would almost force him to stop and pay attention to her.

Again, we are struck by her persistence. This was not a mannerly petition. This was fearless interruption. This was bold insistence.

For the first time in the episode, Jesus explicitly addressed the woman. "It is not good," he said, "to take the children's bread and throw it to the dogs."

This is not one of the verses that we see in embroidered hangings in the church parlor. This doesn't make it onto inspirational posters or into promise boxes. This is not the sort of verse that you are likely to find underlined or highlighted in many Bibles.

The unpleasant line is an extension of Jesus' earlier word about his mission. The "children" evidently represented the covenant people of God — the Jews to whom he was sent. The "bread" represents the ministry and blessings that he had for them. "The dogs," meanwhile, seem to be a reference to the Gentiles. It was a reference to this woman.

We recoil at the seeming racism of the statement. But, again, we mustn't misunderstand what Jesus was saying and doing there. Remember, after all, that on other occasions he abruptly declined to perform a sign for those who demanded one of him. He was not afraid to say a direct *no* to a person. Yet that was not what he was doing there. He was not saying *no*, and he was not sending her away. Instead, it seems that he was challenging her.

This intrepid saint rose to the challenge. "Yes, Lord," she replied, "but even the dogs feed on the crumbs which fall from the master's table." She didn't get bogged down debating or denying the children-dog paradigm. No, she climbed right into it, and still managed to keep asking for him to meet her need.

Jesus' response revealed his pleasure. "O woman," he exclaimed, "your faith is great; be it done for you as you wish." And the narrator told us that the daughter back home was healed instantly.

In the end, you see, the woman got what she came for. She didn't get it easily, and she didn't get it immediately; but she got it. She is, therefore, a model of prayer for us.

How often have we taken "no" for an answer, when we haven't even heard "no"? More than likely, we have had exactly the experience as this woman: we've heard nothing. We've called out and gotten no response. That is discouraging, to be sure, but it's not a "no." Yet that is enough to make so many of us give up and walk away.

She did not. She followed. She called out. She persisted. She annoyed. She even retorted. And when it was all said and done, Jesus himself commended her for her faith, and her need was met.

The disciples came to Jesus one day, saying, "Lord, teach us to pray." If they had made their request on the day they were all walking together in the region around Tyre and Sidon, they wouldn't have needed to look any further than this Gentile woman. Her example was enough to teach them — and us — how to pray.

Amen.

The Personal Question

There's a sign at one point along the Ohio Turnpike that reads, "Divide Between Great Lakes and Mississippi River Watersheds."

You can see similar signs in all sorts of places as you drive around the United States — signs marking continental divides, watersheds, and such. The watershed, of course, is that point of demarcation that divides which way the water flows. At that point on the Ohio Turnpike, for example, all the water on the one side flowed into the Great Lakes, while all the water on the other side flowed into the Mississippi River. A bigger, more significant watershed exists in the Rocky Mountains, where all the water to the east flows, ultimately, into the Atlantic Ocean; while all the water to the west flows into the Pacific.

We might say that Matthew 16:13-20 is a kind of watershed in the gospel story. Everything that happens prior to that episode flows in one direction. Everything that happens after that moment flows in a different direction.

Between the time of his baptism in the Jordan River and his crucifixion in Jerusalem, Jesus had a public ministry that, by most estimates, lasted about three years. Most of those years were spent on and around that scenic lake in northern Israel, the Sea of Galilee. It was there — in those hills, along those shores, and in those villages — that Jesus went about preaching and teaching, healing the sick, and casting out demons. The evidence suggests that Jesus was enjoying a growing popularity and renown, with news about him was spreading for miles. People were coming great distances in order to see him, to hear him, and in many cases to be healed by him. Whatever it was that Jesus had come to do — to accomplish or to conquer — it seemed that he was well on his way there in his Galilean ministry.

But then, into the midst of that happy momentum, Jesus introduced a word of foreboding. For the first time, he told his disciples what he had really come to do, and what that would include. He told them that he was going to Jerusalem, and that there he would be apprehended by the leaders of the people, who would hand him over to be tortured and executed.

From that moment on, everything began to flow toward Jerusalem. Everything began to point toward the cross. The hinge — the watershed — between those happy early days in Galilee and the events leading up to Christ's passion and crucifixion in Jerusalem was this episode at the town of Caesarea Philippi.

It was there, at that pivotal event, that Jesus asked his disciples a question. He asked a personal question.

As we read the stories of scripture, we see that this was a recurring pattern. From the Garden of Eden on, the Lord was continually asking questions of people. But these were not the sort of questions that a person asks out of ignorance — like questions we might ask about how to do something or where to find something. No, the Lord does not ask us questions because he needs to know the answer; he asks us questions because *we* need to know the answer. We need to know the answers, and we need to say those answers.

In this way, the Lord's questions are like the sorts of questions that both parents and teachers typically ask of children. It's not the parent who needs to know what to say in a certain circumstance; it's the child. Yet the parent asks, "Now what do you say?" as a prompt so that the child will know and will say the correct answer. Likewise, the teacher does not need the student to tell him or her in what year the Declaration of Independence was signed. The teacher asks the question in order to guarantee that the student knows the answer.

So it was that, there at Caesarea Philippi, Jesus asked his disciples a question. But, like the parent or the teacher, Jesus does ask the question to learn, but to teach. He asked, "Who do people say that I am?"

As you read the story, you get the feeling that the disciples didn't hesitate to answer that question. After all, it must have been very exciting for those men to be part of the inner circle around the one who was so popular, so famous, and so powerful. Jesus was the center of growing attention, and the disciples were close to that center. Surely, therefore, they had heard so much talk, rumors, and speculation about Jesus. And more than just hearing the speculation of the crowds, the disciples must have talked about it amongst themselves, as well.

When Jesus asked the question, therefore, the disciples knew all the answers. We imagine them talking over one another as they tried to repeat all the gossip they had heard. "I heard someone say that they thought you were John the Baptist come back to life!" "Yes, I've heard that, too…. I heard someone else say that you were Elijah." "Or Jeremiah," another called out. "I heard someone say that he was sure you were one of the prophets of old, but he wasn't sure which one yet."

They might have gone on, back and forth, sharing the stories, repeating the rumors, relishing the scuttlebutt. It's all very heady stuff. The disciples had no doubt heard a great deal of speculation about who Jesus was, and so they were eager and able to answer that question,

But then Jesus asked them another question. A second question. A personal question.

"What about *you*?" he asked. "Who do *you* say that I am?"

As you read the episode, you get the sense that this second question quieted down the group. No excited hubbub anymore. There was no tripping over one another to blurt out answers. Instead, for at least a moment, it was perhaps uncomfortably quiet.

You know the look and feel of a group where everyone is reluctant to answer. You know the anxiety that comes with being the first one to talk. So it is that the disciples looked at one another, or at the ground: everyone was just a bit afraid to answer.

There are, you see, at least two risks in answering the personal question that Jesus had asked. First, of course, there is the simple risk of being incorrect — of being the guy who said, "This is who I believe you are," only to have Jesus say, "No, you're wrong. That's not who I am."

We should pause to mention that, in our relativistic culture, we have almost entirely lost sight of this particular risk. We have so broadly bought into the notion that each individual may believe whatever he or she wants to about Jesus that we no longer consider the risk of being wrong, of him having to say, "No, that's not who I am."

The first risk that the disciples felt was the risk of being wrong. And then this other matter — in addition to the risk of being wrong — there was the risk of being radical.

There is, in almost every group, a certain paralysis that comes from wondering what the others will think. What if what I say seems to them stupid or outlandish? What if it is laughable or ridiculous? We imagine the disciples standing there, quietly fidgeting, with no one saying anything.

Except Peter.

Peter: the disciple most likely to pop up and say something or do something, whether he should or not. Peter, you recall, was the one who clumsily broke into the Transfiguration scene with a silly suggestion about building three tabernacles. Peter was the one who wanted to climb out of the boat and go to Jesus on the water. Peter was the one who piped up and objected when Jesus tried to wash his feet. Peter was the one who boldly proclaimed his though-none-go-with-me faithfulness at the Last Supper, and then just as vigorously denied that he knew Jesus a few hours later.

On this occasion, while none of the other disciples was saying anything, Peter piped up and said something. "Thou art the Christ," Peter declared; "the Son of the living God!"

There were two risks: the risk of being wrong, and the risk of being radical. Peter was radical, but Peter was not wrong.

Jesus said, "Peter, you are right! And furthermore I want you to know that flesh and blood has not revealed this to you, but rather my Father in heaven!"

All the earlier answers, you see, were flesh and blood answers: human speculation, popular scuttlebutt. But Peter's personal answer to Jesus' personal question: that didn't come from other people; it came from God.

That's an interesting phenomenon, isn't it? The question came from God, and the answer came from God.

We noted earlier this provocative phenomenon that we see across the pages of scripture: the Lord asked people questions. He asked questions of Adam and Eve, of Cain, of Sarah, of Jacob, of Moses, of Elijah, of Ezekiel, and on and on. Each question had its own unique circumstance and context, yet it may be that a thoughtful consideration of God's questions would reveal that they have a timeless quality to them.

We read, for example, that the Lord asked Sarah, "Is anything too difficult for the Lord?" (Genesis 18:14). The question came from over three thousand years ago, yet we recognize that the relevance and impact of that question is not limited to Sarah's time and situation. Perhaps the Lord continues to ask us if we think something is too hard for him. Perhaps that is a question we need to answer.

Likewise, the question that Jesus asked his disciples that day by Caesarea Philippi — the personal question — "Who do *you* say that I am?"

Just like that first group of disciples, we live in a world where we are surrounded by speculation about Jesus. Some of it is reverent, some unintentionally trivializing, and some of it deliberately antagonistic. In the midst of a world of speculators, head-scratchers, and opponents, Jesus turned to the people who knew him — the ones closest to him, the ones who followed him — and he said to them and to us, "What about you? Who do you say that I am?"

By your words and by your life, who do you say that he is? Do you say that he is ancient history or present reality? Do you say that he is just one among many in the pages of history and just one among many priorities in your life? Or do your words and life say that he is God's only Son, your only Lord, and the world's only hope and Savior?

Let us admit that Jesus' question would be a much easier one if it were a slightly different one. If he had asked, "Who do you think that I am" or even "Who do you believe that I am," the answer would be an easier one. But that's not what he asked.

"Who do you say...?" That was his question. "Who do you *say* that I am?" Like the child under the instruction of his parent or the student under the instruction of her teacher, the believer needs to know — and needs to say — the answer.

Here's an interesting fact. Three of the four gospels tell us about this incident, and one of those three gospel writers, Matthew, was probably there at the time. Yet there is no indication of what the other disciples felt or thought. We don't know if they were thinking along the same lines as Peter or if they were way off track. We don't know if they were surprised by Peter's response or by Jesus' affirmation of it. Peter was the only one who stuck his neck out and said something — said something about Jesus — while none of the other disciples there did. As a result, this passage has become known as "Peter's declaration about Christ." Whether they were right or wrong about Jesus, the other disciples did not speak up, and in the end, they were not really notable here. The moment belonged to Peter.

I wonder if that's not how all of history will one day be written and remembered. For, you see, Jesus Christ is the great watershed. He is the line along which everything is divided. His first coming divided history in two — before and after. His second coming will divide all of humanity in two — with him or without him, for him or against him.

For the time being, the world shines its spotlight on those who are powerful and important, those who start wars or win wars, those who make the big impact politically, militarily, economically, scientifically, or even culturally. But in the end, when heaven's spotlight outshines and makes dim all of the rest, I suspect we will discover that the most notable thing about every individual's life will be this: What they said, or what they did not say, about Jesus Christ.

Elections and thrones, wars and economies, headlines and borders, careers and net worth — all this stuff will wither into insignificance when set next to one question. It is the personal question, the watershed question: "Who do *you* say that he is?"

Amen.

www.ingramcontent.com/pod-product-compliance
Lightning Source LLC
LaVergne TN
LVHW091202080426
835509LV00006B/797